The
Cleveland
Clinic Way

The
Cleveland
Clinic Way

LESSONS IN EXCELLENCE FROM
ONE OF THE WORLD'S LEADING
HEALTHCARE ORGANIZATIONS

Toby Cosgrove, MD

President and CEO of Cleveland Clinic

NEW YORK   CHICAGO   SAN FRANCISCO
ATHENS   LONDON   MADRID
MEXICO CITY   MILAN   NEW DELHI
SINGAPORE   SYDNEY   TORONTO

4 5 6 7 8 9 0   DOC/DOC   1 9 8 7 6 5 4

ISBN: 978-0-07-182724-9
MHID: 0-07-182724-2

e-ISBN: 978-0-07-182725-6
e-MHID: 0-07-182725-0

Design by Lee Fukui and Mauna Eichner

Library of Congress Cataloging-in-Publication Data

Cosgrove, Toby, 1940-
   The Cleveland Clinic way : lessons in excellence from one of the world's leading health care organizations / by Toby Cosgrove, MD.
      pages cm
   ISBN 978-0-07-182724-9 (alk. paper) — ISBN 0-07-182724-2 (alk. paper)
1. Cleveland Clinic Foundation. 2. Health facilities—Standards—United States—Ohio. 3. Integrative medicine—United States--Ohio.. I. Title.
   RA982.C6C67 2014
   362.1109771—dc23

                                                        2013038181

McGraw-Hill Education books are available at special quantity discounts to use as premiums and sales promotions or for use in corporate training programs. To contact a representative, please visit the Contact Us pages at www .mhprofessional.com.

To all Cleveland Clinic caregivers,

past and present, and to

the patients who have trusted us

with their care

Contents

Preface

Terri McCort was expecting a baby.[1] She was already five days overdue. As she sat down for dinner, she felt an unusual pain at the base of her throat. She didn't know it, but she was in mortal danger. Deep inside her chest, the largest blood vessel in her body, the aorta, was beginning to tear itself apart. If left untreated, it would rupture massively, gushing blood like an open fire hydrant. Terri and her unborn baby would die.

Terri was hard to ignore as she burst through the doors of her local emergency room. She was tall and long-armed like Abraham Lincoln. And, as has been speculated about Lincoln, Terri has Marfan syndrome, a genetic disease of the connective tissue that can render the aorta fatally fragile. The disease had already killed her father and three brothers. Now it seemed like it was Terri's turn.

Fortunately, the caregivers at Terri's southern Ohio hospital knew exactly what to do in the case of a complex emergency that was unlike anything they'd ever seen: they called Cleveland Clinic.

A helicopter arrived and flew Terri to Cleveland Clinic's advanced care facilities. With her condition worsening by the minute, a multispecialty team that included a surgeon, a cardiologist, and an obstetrician went to work. They stabilized her and assessed her condition. She was rushed to an operating room, where her aorta was clamped and she was placed on a heart-lung machine. The obstetrician stepped in and performed an emergency cesarean to deliver a beautiful baby boy.

As Terri's baby was being examined, the heart and vascular team surrounded the table. Aortic rescue can be dangerous. It includes some of the most complex procedures in all of cardiovascular surgery. Few specialists anywhere have experience in the full range of techniques required. Terri's team of surgeons, anesthesiologists, technicians, and nurses went to work. They knew that it would be a long night, but they were determined that Terri would live to see her newborn son the next day.

If Terri's local hospital hadn't sent her to Cleveland Clinic, she probably wouldn't have made it through the night. "We were racing against the clock," said one of the surgeons. But Terri got to see her son the next day, and after nine days in the hospital, she was able to go home. She spent the next four months recovering, but eventually she went back to work as an inspector at a basket factory. Her son, Seth, is now in his early twenties. A "typical young man," in Terri's words, he enjoys computers and spending time with his girlfriend. He also has Marfan syndrome and goes for annual checks of his aorta.

Terri's case exemplifies the virtues of a unique model of medicine—a system in which caregivers work as a team, doctors purely practice medicine, and the patient comes first. Unlike the majority of American physicians, those at Cleveland Clinic and a few other institutions aren't free agents who are affiliated with a specific hospital. They are employees of the same organization that owns the hospital, and they practice as an integrated group—behind-the-scenes facts that make a huge difference. In Terri's case, top experts in a dozen fields were able to scramble in the middle of the night to pull off a complex and unusual medical intervention. It was a seamless collaboration and the kind of "everyday miracle" that has captured the attention of everyone from the president of the United States to the *New Yorker*.

We all know that American healthcare is supposed to be a mess. Yet on the frontiers of medicine, Cleveland Clinic has developed an approach to treating people that is more effective, more humane, and, surprisingly, more affordable. By reorganizing doctors and other caregivers so that they work together better and by reorienting medical institutions in ways that embrace and enhance collaboration, innovation, patient experience, and wellness, we could solve all kinds of problems—including financial ones—that are driving our ominous healthcare "crisis." We could help individuals live longer, healthier lives without bankrupting the nation. We could launch a technology revolution that would save lives. We could make visits to the hospital more pleasant and emotionally healing experiences. And we could help doctors engage with patients and with one another as people and enjoy the practice of medicine again.

As CEO of Cleveland Clinic, I lead a multibillion-dollar enterprise that has outposts around the world. But I wasn't born a CEO. I spent most of my career in the medical trenches as a cardiac surgeon, performing more than 22,000 operations, including the world's first minimally invasive valve surgery. Instruments and techniques that I invented are used in operating rooms everywhere. I know the sights, sounds, and smells of the operating room. I know what it takes to build a small, tight-knit team for surgery and what it's like to organize an entire system of hospitals. I also know the human side of healthcare. I've felt the thrill of saving a life—not once, but hundreds, even thousands of times. And I understand what it's like to lose a patient and then have to face the family in the waiting room.

I love my patients and I love being a doctor, but I've never felt like a medical insider. I finished at the bottom of my class in medical school, and I was strongly advised *not* to go into cardiac surgery. I didn't know it at the time, but I had an undiagnosed learning disability: dyslexia. Over the course of my career, this condition has proved to be a blessing in disguise. Because of the limitations it imposed, I never fell prey to the herd mentality. I had to forge my own way of learning about and understanding what went on around me. That informs how I lead Cleveland Clinic.

Across America, people have been asking, "What's wrong with the healthcare system? How do we fix it? What is the best model of healthcare for these times?"

It's clear that some parts of American healthcare are dysfunctional. Other parts seem to work very well. Among the latter are large, not-for-profit group practices such as Cleveland Clinic. The national media have taken note and produced features and articles. President Barack Obama praised Cleveland Clinic and similar organizations on national television and visited us to find out more about how we operate. The level of interest in this organization and its methods has remained high over the years. People would like to know more about Cleveland Clinic and what we do differently.

The Cleveland Clinic Way arose out of the ongoing national debate on healthcare reform. Our purpose is to share the good news about American healthcare and show how Cleveland Clinic and similar organizations are shaping the future of medicine. This book draws upon my speeches, writings, blog posts, and published Cleveland Clinic communications to provide the most comprehensive and accurate account possible of the subject matter and the organization. Cleveland Clinic has kindly allowed me to quote verbatim and without attribution from authorized publications and corporate communications. The final product is a combination of my thoughts and the wisdom of Cleveland Clinic caregivers, past and present.

It's a positive vision of healthcare compared with the ones that we usually see. And it's a vision that I hope will shift not only how we as medical professionals talk about medicine but how we practice it—and how we lead our healthcare organizations, empowering citizens to make more informed decisions about their health and reigniting pride in American medicine and American innovation.

The Cleveland Clinic Way isn't about the complexities of the health insurance debate. It doesn't take a stand on the specifics of recent healthcare legislation, nor does it talk about how individual doctors should treat individual diseases. Rather, it's an overview of how our dominant system of practicing medicine can be over-hauled for the better, giving a look at a healthcare revolution that is already under way at Cleveland Clinic—and is one that we need to further and hasten. Ultimately, I hope you'll find it an inspiring book about how real doctors could intervene in new ways to better the lives of real people.

People like Terri McCort. People like you.

Acknowledgments

Teamwork is part of everything we do at Cleveland Clinic. This book is no exception. My deepest gratitude goes to the patients and families who shared their inspiring stories with us. May you always enjoy the best of health.

Thank you as well to all the doctors and administrators who took time out of their busy schedules to be interviewed and, in some cases, to read through chapters of the manuscript. Your assistance was invaluable. In particular, I would like to thank Dr. Jim Merlino, chief experience officer of Cleveland Clinic, and Dr. Jim Young, chair of the Endocrinology & Metabolism Institute and executive dean of the Cleveland Clinic Lerner College of Medicine, for taking the time to review the manuscript and offer helpful suggestions and comments.

Linda McHugh, executive administrator of Cleveland Clinic, oversaw the project from beginning to end with good sense and good judgment. Helen Rees, our literary agent, found a home for the project and shepherded it to completion. Steve Szilagyi, marketing communications, and Seth Schulman of the Providence Word and Thought Company provided editorial assistance. Thank you to each of them. Finally, I would like to thank my wife, Anita, for her patience and support in this and all my endeavors.

I would like to acknowledge the following people by name for having made this book possible: Dr. Stephen Abfall, Barb Ackerman, Ansleigh and Crystal Adkins, Sue Andrella, Beth Armstrong,

Darlene Ballantine, Guido Bergomi, Dr. Gene Blackstone, Dr. Brian Bolwell, Dr. George Thomas Budd, Natoma Canfield, Tony Carosella, Chris Coburn, Joanne Cohen, John Cromer, Connie Culp, Dr. Nina Desai, Megan Doerr, Bill Donato, Dr. Charis Eng, Dr. Tomasso Falcone, Dr. Kathy Franco, Dr. Mark Froimson, Steve Glass, Dr. Eiran Gorodeski, Dr. Tom Graham, Dr. Joe Hahn, Dr. C. Martin Harris, Iyaad Hasan, Dr. Michael Henderson, Beth Hertz, Matthew Hiznay, Dr. Shazam Hussain, Ann Huston, Dr. Joseph Iannotti, David Jesse, Maria Jukic, Dr. Matthew Kalady, Dr. Michael Kattan, Dr. Eric Klein, Pastor Patrick Kleitz, Dr. Deepak Lachhwani, Dr. Sara Lappe, Dr. Bret Lashner, Dr. David Levin, Dr. David Longworth, Doug Lyons, Paul Matsen, Tabitha McClendon, Terri McCort, Stephen McHale, Rosemary and Connor Menneto, Dr. Jim Merlino, Dr. Michael Modic, Dr. William Morris, Jeanne Murphy, Dr. Imad Najm, Dana and Grant Osborne, Jean Parrish, Dr. Shannon Phillips, Carol Reid, Dr. Michael Roizen, Dr. Eric Roselli, Rachel Rusnak, Dr. Maria Siemionow, Dr. Nicholas Smedira, Dr. Daniel Sullivan, Dr. Sharon Sutherlan, Dr. Katherine Teng, Dr. Geoff Vince, Darrell White, David Whiteley, Dr. Robert Wyllie, Dr. James Young, and Stephanie Zimmerman.

Group Practices Provide Better—and Cheaper—Care

Winter in Cleveland can be beautiful when the air is crisp and the evergreens are cloaked in white. But by mid-March, with its bare trees and gray skies, a longing for something more alive fills the air. Against this backdrop, Lisa Cantwell, a woman in her thirties, saw her doctor for a prenatal ultrasound. Already the mother of two young children, she had been through prenatal testing before. But nothing could have prepared her for the ordeal that she and her husband, Josh, were about to face.

The ultrasound, performed at 18 weeks, showed something in the baby's neck—a dark mass, six centimeters across. In 35 years, Lisa's prenatal specialist had never seen anything like it.

Several follow-up scans that spring and summer revealed that the cyst was growing. Lisa's caregivers were concerned that the cyst would impair the baby's ability to breathe. Her case was transferred from Cleveland Clinic's community hospital to the main campus, which handles the most serious medical cases. Mother and child were admitted to the Fetal Care Center, where a multidisciplinary team of obstetricians, neonatologists, and pediatric subspecialists would provide care. The center is not a place but a virtual team linked by purpose, protocols, and electronic medical records.

When the time came for Lisa to give birth, Dr. Paul Krakowitz, a leading pediatric head and neck surgeon, discovered that the mass was just under the baby's windpipe. The baby might not be able to breathe outside the uterus. Cutting the umbilical cord could prove fatal.

Dr. Krakowitz's team used a rare procedure. Two operating rooms were prepared side by side. Surgeons waited in the second room, ready to operate on the baby if needed. In the first room, Lisa had a normal cesarean, but the baby was lifted only partially out of the uterus. Before full birth, Dr. Krakowitz performed an endoscopy to see whether the baby's windpipe was clear. It was. Baby Dominic was fully delivered and sent to the Neonatal Intensive Care Unit.

To the naked eye, the baby's neck looked perfectly normal, but the cyst was under the skin—and growing. It was a cystic hygroma, a large sac filled with fluid. Once they were home, Lisa carefully monitored Dominic to ensure that the cyst didn't impede his breathing. Almost every day, she checked in by phone with the nurse who ran the Fetal Care Center. But in the second week, Lisa noticed that Dominic was turning blue. The cyst had grown so big that it was strangling her son.

Lisa and Josh rushed Dominic to Cleveland Clinic's Emergency Department. Doctors intubated Dominic to open his airway, and Dr. Krakowitz prepared to operate. The next day, he removed a cyst running from the left lobe of the thyroid into the cervical spine, up through the thyroid cartilage, and into one of the tubes that connect the nasal cavity to the ears. These structures are tiny in a two-week-old infant, and the cranial nerves that control hearing and speech run through them. Bleeding had to be controlled because babies don't have much blood to begin with. The operation, which took 4½ hours, was a success. Dominic was moved to the Pediatric Intensive Care Unit, where additional medical specialists and highly trained nurses stabilized him. He was on the road to recovery and a normal life.

How Doctors Are Organized Matters

No single person saved Dominic's life. His survival lay in the hands of many caregivers—highly skilled specialists who included radiologists, otolaryngologists, neonatologists, obstetricians, anesthesiologists, nurses, and technicians. The caregivers who treated Dominic were an integrated group, with each function supporting every other function. Every circuit was connected, from the top medical specialist to the nurses to the blue-scrubs team that disinfected the operating rooms. Like any tightly knit team in the corporate world, Dominic's caregivers all wore the same logo, reported up the same organizational chart, and had the same signature on their paychecks. They also had the same mission: to save lives, put patients first, and advance the cause of health and medicine. And as members of a group practice, they had the protection of quality and safety protocols, cost efficiencies in purchasing, and a commitment to innovation and process improvement.

For all the talk about America's healthcare "system," it's not a system at all. There are about 800,000 doctors in the United States.[1] Some of these doctors are self-employed. Some work for hospitals. Many work in practices of fewer than 20 colleagues. As of 2012, about 40 percent were truly independent.[2] This small-scale, cottage-industry approach can deliver finely crafted services, but the quality of those services is variable, and costs are typically high. Coordination, standardization, quality improvement, and all the other factors that today make high-quality products and services available to more people more rapidly and more cheaply than at any other time in history have yet to be generally implemented in healthcare.

However, the same strategies that have revolutionized every industry from textile manufacturing to farming over the past 250 years can be applied to healthcare. The first step is to organize doctors differently—to bring them together to form much larger organizations led by doctors, not professional managers.

In 2005, only 4.5 percent of American doctors worked in group practices of 50 or more.[3] But this is rapidly changing. More of American healthcare undoubtedly will shift to the group practice model embraced by the Mayo Clinic, the Cleveland Clinic, Kaiser Permanente (California), and similar organizations. We will probably see more and more groupings of hundreds, even thousands, of physicians. These groups invariably will—and should—embrace a corporate model, paying doctors a salary, tying continued employment and raises to annual performance reviews, and leveraging their size to buy high-quality equipment and supplies more cheaply.

Origins of the Group Practice Model and Cleveland Clinic

The group practice model was essentially born in the midwestern United States. The first nonprofit group practice was established by William and Charlie Mayo in Rochester, Minnesota, more than 100 years ago. Today, Mayo Clinic is the largest nonprofit group practice in the world. The second largest is Cleveland Clinic, founded in 1921. The founders of Cleveland Clinic—George Crile Sr., Frank Bunts, William Lower, and John Phillips—were good friends with the Mayo brothers. They hunted and fished together, stayed at one another's homes, and shared ideas on the best way to organize the practice of medicine.[4] These doctors, led by Dr. Crile, were among the first physicians to volunteer when America entered the Great War in 1917. Dr. Crile and his colleagues set up military hospitals not far from the front. They were impressed by the military approach to medicine, which was so different from the private practice model that dominated civilian medicine. Military medicine was collective. Supplies were managed efficiently. Innovations were adopted quickly. Everyone shared the same mission, and all were focused on the patient and making the patient better.[5]

When Dr. Crile and his colleagues returned to Cleveland, they saw an opportunity to create an ideal medical center. They wanted to start with a blank slate and apply the lessons of the Mayo Clinic and military medicine to create a new kind of medical enterprise. Thus was born Cleveland Clinic.

Nonprofit

We are a nonprofit group practice. Nobody owns Cleveland Clinic. We are a community trust.

Board of Directors

At the top of the organization is an elected board of directors. The board oversees our nonprofit mission, approves budgets, sets compensation, and manages property transfers. The board includes business leaders, philanthropic leaders, and community-minded individuals.

CEO and President

Next is the CEO, who is also president of the board. The CEO sets policies in collaboration with an executive team and oversees the administration of all clinical and operational activities. The CEO communicates the organization's progress to caregivers, along with its mission, vision, and values.

Chief of Staff

The chief of staff manages all affairs relating to the employment of Cleveland Clinic's medical staff.

Staff Physicians and Scientists

Cleveland Clinic has 3,000 salaried physicians and scientists on staff. These professionals represent 120 medical specialties and sub-specialties. All are on one-year contracts and are subject to annual performance reviews.

Support and Services

Cleveland Clinic's medical staff is supported by more than 40,000 caregivers, including 11,000 nurses. These caregivers include allied health professionals, administrators, clerical workers, maintenance personnel, information technology experts, financial experts, billing and appointment-making personnel, and hundreds of other job categories. All contribute to the patient care experience.

Cleveland Clinic is a physician-run organization. This is a big distinction. There are good arguments for the lay administration of some types of medical centers. But more than 90 years of experience has convinced us that physician leadership is best for a non-profit group practice. Doctors bear the ultimate responsibility for the health and well-being of their patients, so it makes sense that doctors, rather than laypersons, make the decisions about the functional activities that surround patient care. At Cleveland Clinic, a physician CEO and president, a physician board of governors, physician chairs of institutes, and other physician leaders make key decisions for the organization (albeit with the advice and consent of a lay board of directors and in collaboration with nurses, scientists, and lay administrators at every level). The authority granted to doctors may be one of the reasons that Cleveland Clinic physicians score so well on employee engagement surveys: their collective power is commensurate with their responsibilities. The judgment of medical experts ensures that every policy and procedure implemented serves the goal of providing patients with the best care possible.

Arguments for and Against the Group Practice Model

If the group practice model is so effective, why aren't there more group practices? Doctors resist the group practice model for the same reason that the Green Mountain Boys resisted the British: they like their independence. The medical profession attracts smart, capable, self-driven individuals. They can and do enjoy successful careers managing their own affairs in private practice.

Traditionally, hospitals are not expected to lead healthcare. Rather, they serve as a doctors' workshop, where physicians can make decisions about their patients' care without bureaucratic encumbrance. One historian noted that when recognizably modern hospitals first emerged in the late nineteenth and early twentieth centuries, "the physician hierarchy and organization was separate from the administrative hierarchy and organization."[6] This still holds true in many hospitals today.

Patient preference also plays a role. The memory of the country doctor who travels from house call to house call with a black bag is cherished, as is the Norman Rockwell image of the kindly practitioner taking a patient's pulse with a pocket watch.

Given these entrenched views, the founders of early group practices were not popular with the medical establishment of their day. They were called "medical Soviets," "Bolsheviks," and "communistic."[7] Professional associations railed against what they termed the "corporate practice of medicine." When some physicians in Palo Alto, California, attempted to start a group practice, they were barred from their local medical association.[8] The American Medical Association countered the growing menace of the group practice by publishing a reaffirmation of what it believed were the key principles of the medical profession: solo practice, fee-based compensation, individual physician control over the services provided, and "the conviction that medical institutions are but logistical extensions of physician practice."[9] In Northeast Ohio in the 1920s, the local medical powers were so alarmed by the prospect of a group practice in their midst that they threatened the founders of Cleveland Clinic with the loss of admitting privileges at local hospitals. In response, the Cleveland Clinic group built its own hospital, which has since grown to a 1,300-bed complex on its original site.

Good arguments on both sides of the group practice controversy existed then, just as they do now. Many people believe that the group practice model sullies the doctor-patient relationship, making doctors more beholden to the organization than to the patient. Some can't shake the idea that giving doctors salaries leads to inattentive care. The laws and regulations governing medicine also tend to favor the private practice model. Some state legislatures have passed measures prohibiting the corporate practice of medicine. In its early days, Cleveland Clinic had to take complex legal roundabouts simply to collect fees and distribute salaries to doctors.[10]

But the group practice pioneers also had their champions. In 1932, a committee of enlightened medical reformers declared that "[m]any of the difficulties in present medical practice can be overcome, wholly or in part, by group organization."[11]

The recent national debate on healthcare reform, leading to the Patient Protection and Affordable Care Act being signed into law in 2010, thrust the group practice model back into the spotlight. Today, the group practice model has supporters at the highest levels of government. In 2008, for example, President Barack Obama told a national television audience that Cleveland Clinic, Mayo Clinic, and similar practices "offer some of the highest quality of care in the nation, at some of the lowest costs in the nation."[12] Four years later, both President Obama and Governor Mitt Romney mentioned Cleveland Clinic approvingly in their first presidential debate, on October 3, 2012.

Still, resistance among doctors dies hard. It's not easy to cast off the Lone Ranger mentality. Some doctors continue to believe that their individual brilliance will be stifled in a collaborative setting. Others maintain that getting doctors to agree and work together is a hopeless task. Dr. Harry Hartzell, a retired pediatrician from the Palo Alto Medical Foundation, once said, "Three types of people don't get along in a group: the hard-driving entrepreneur who wants to create an empire; someone who always wants to have a minority opinion; and a person who doesn't like to discuss issues, negotiate and compromise."[13]

There are good arguments on both sides. But the success of Cleveland Clinic, Mayo Clinic, the Palo Alto Medical Foundation, and other group practices testifies to the value of this model in delivering exceptional and efficient care.

Measuring Exceptional Care

Excellent outcomes such as Dominic Cantwell's are the rule, not the exception, for large medical groups, as evidenced in part by published outcomes and rankings by reputation or quality. The Centers for Medicare & Medicaid Services publishes a number of quality and safety indicators for hospitals on its website, cms.gov.

Another widely acknowledged and frequently cited measure of overall hospital and specialty quality is the annual *U.S. News & World Report* "Best Hospitals" rankings. *U.S. News* factors in a variety of measures, from reputation to mortality rate to nurse-patient ratio, to arrive at its conclusions. The large group practices are disproportionately represented at the very top—Mayo Clinic and Cleveland Clinic are regularly ranked among the top four hospitals in America. Intermountain Healthcare's Intermountain Medical Center is ranked the top hospital in Utah, and its LDS Hospital ranks third. In 2013–14, Cleveland Clinic was ranked number one in America for cardiac care for the 19th year in a row, and number two in urology, nephrology, diabetes and endocrinology, digestive diseases, and rheumatology. Mayo Clinic was number one in five specialties. It seems fair to conclude from these results that large group practices must be doing something right.

General rankings are one thing, but where are the more specific studies of the underlying data? In truth, accurate, direct comparisons are hard to come by. One of the drawbacks of independent practices is that they are unlikely to measure, record, or share their outcomes as diligently as the big groups do.

A few studies have tackled this problem. One comparison found that patients at multispecialty group practices received care that was 15 percent higher in quality than the care that patients received at nongroup practices.[14] Another study looked at care management processes, which are structured procedures for treating specific conditions or diseases; they establish core treatment plans around which doctors can individualize care. Having care management processes in place makes for better outcomes. This study found that large multispecialty group practices were more likely to have such processes in place for asthma, congestive heart failure, depression, and diabetes.[15]

If physician groups do indeed perform better, the question is why. Much of the answer is based on how they enhance collaboration, benchmarking, innovation, the patient experience, convenience, and personalized healthcare. An even more basic, commonsense reason is this: group practices have an easier time measuring and improving care.

Improving Care

How can the performance of an entity as large and complex as a hospital be improved, given that there are so many different professionals coming together to get the job done? How can doctors, nurses, technicians, and other support staff improve, for instance, the care that lung transplant patients receive so that they recover more quickly and stay in intensive care for fewer days? How can the many teams within a hospital uniformly sterilize surgical instruments so that patients sustain fewer serious infections? How can teams of professionals—each with different training and perspectives—

improve their care of women during labor and delivery to mini-mize the number of risky procedures (for example, cesarean sec-tions) that these women undergo?

In business and manufacturing, quality improvement is a way of life. Leaders push managers and line employees to work together in new ways to overcome the inertia of "the way we've always done it." Unfortunately, the business-as-usual model has particular stay-ing power in healthcare. When individuals and groups of doctors have little connection to the centralized hospital leadership—when they have their own fiefdoms of power and influence—it can be ex-tremely difficult to agree on changes and to coordinate key play-ers enough to make change happen. In the usual model, the leaders of various departments continually worry about their budgets be-ing slashed or their authority being undermined. An Institute of Medicine report put it well: "In the current system, care is taken to protect professional prerogatives and separate roles. The current system shows too little cooperation and teamwork. Instead, each discipline and type of organization tends to defend its authority at the expense of the total system's function."[16]

In a large, physician-run group practice, in which everyone works for one organization, quality improvement initiatives can be launched with minimal friction because the employees share common goals. Additionally, at physician-run group practices, the caregivers are held responsible *as individuals* (for example, through yearly performance reviews) for how well they're meeting perfor-mance goals, especially the care they provide to patients. Here is an example of how continuously improving the delivery of healthcare has helped patients at Cleveland Clinic.

A six-year-old girl brought to one of Cleveland Clinic's hospi-tal emergency departments late at night was suffering from acute pneumonia, which causes inflammation of the lungs and is partic-ularly dangerous for patients who are either very old or very young. A child with acute pneumonia may suddenly be unable to breathe normally. It is urgent that such a child be placed on mechanical ventilation under the supervision of qualified caregivers in a properly equipped intensive care unit.

In this case, the Emergency Department stabilized the girl and sent her to Cleveland Clinic Children's, where we have a leading-edge Pediatric Intensive Care Unit (PICU). The PICU is staffed 24 hours a day with two respiratory therapists and a pediatric intensivist (an intensive care doctor who specializes in treating children). These caregivers were able to intervene rapidly and prevent the girl's potentially fatal condition from worsening.

Having a pediatric intensivist on duty 24/7 used to be unheard of. That changed in 1996, when Cleveland Clinic became the first PICU in the country to have one. Following implementation of the 24/7 coverage, Cleveland Clinic's PICU survival rate rose to 98 percent, a full 2 percentage points higher than the national average. That means that 2 kids out of 100 who wouldn't survive in other PICUs would survive in ours.[17]

The group practice structure enabled us to test the validity of this staffing initiative and, once it was proven, to implement it at all the PICUs across our various facilities with few problems.

Continuous improvement is the norm at Cleveland Clinic. Currently, our doctors are leading initiatives to drive down rates of readmission, pressure ulcers, and hospital-acquired infections and to reduce "never events" (things that simply shouldn't happen in a hospital) to zero. We have established best practices to avoid central line–associated bloodstream infections and put together a hospitalwide team dedicated to educating caregivers on proper line insertion, maintenance, and removal. By applying these steps, we've been able to reduce infections from catheters by 40 percent and urinary tract infections by 50 percent.[18]

In 2010, we gathered together every caregiver involved in lung transplantation for a step-by-step analysis of our lung transplant program to see if we could get even better results by improving teamwork. We streamlined processes, eliminated redundant tasks, and pared every last bit of procedural fat. A year later, not only were patients getting home faster, but they were living longer. The length of a hospital stay had been reduced by 7 percent, or 1.5 days, and we had improved 30-day survival rates to 97 percent from 94 percent the year before.[19]

Imagine replicating that plan across specialties, with similar medical outcomes—from how epilepsy patients are cared for to how babies are delivered to how patients who need prostate surgery are treated. As a culture of continuous improvement begins to take shape, the hospital becomes a very different place.

Cleveland Clinic is hardly the only large group practice that is making strides in improving quality. It's happening all over the country. At Geisinger Health System in Pennsylvania, cardiac surgeons collaborated to develop best practices for coronary artery bypass surgery. They created protocols, tools, and reminders and made sure that staff members used them. The result? The number of coronary artery bypass patients dying on the operating table fell by 67 percent, and the average hospital stay for patients following surgery decreased by more than a day.[20]

Orthopedists at Kaiser Permanente created a program to identify and treat people who were more likely to have osteoporosis and hip fractures. They implemented numerous changes, such as increased testing, increased use of preventive medicines, and standard guidelines for managing osteoporosis. Over the course of five years, hip fractures in at-risk patients declined by 50 percent.[21]

At Intermountain Healthcare, doctors realized that the practice of inducing labor early led to higher complication rates. Intermountain convened a team of specialists that created a standard checklist for determining when doctors should induce labor and distributed that checklist throughout the organization. Patients who met the criteria were induced; others who didn't could still be induced, but only with special approval from a top specialist. As a result, the number of babies born to women who chose to induce fell, as did the number of babies who were admitted to newborn intensive care units. Although 34 percent of deliveries nationwide take place by cesarean section, at Intermountain only 21 percent of deliveries take this path. Less induction, fewer complications, better-quality care—all because doctors were able to work together to improve what they're doing in basic ways.[22]

Each of these examples demonstrates that better care doesn't come from implementing some radically new equipment or pathbreaking medicine—it comes from caregivers paying closer attention to what they are doing, using what they already know to design better ways of treating patients, and putting systems in place so that people actually change their behavior.

Improving care is fundamentally an *organizational* issue. Unfortunately, one survey of doctors nationwide found that only a third reported that they had helped redesign the system of care in their hospital to improve performance.[23] If doctors everywhere can begin to work together better, the way they do in large group practices, to improve patient care, satisfaction, and outcomes, a dynamic paradigm will emerge that puts the focus in healthcare where it belongs—on the patient.

Putting Patients First

Patients instinctively know that the best doctors are those who see them as people rather than as numbers. These are the doctors who think through each patient's situation carefully to determine the treatments or interventions that would be best for *that individual*— the doctors who put patients *first*, ahead of concerns about money, insurance, or other issues related to the practice of medicine.

Talented, empathetic, caring, skilled physicians exist at every institution in America. Some of these physicians are free agents, some practice in small groups organized around a specialty, and some practice in large, physician-run group practices. At large group practices, however, doctors are in a much better position to listen to patients and treat them without the concerns that often weigh on other physicians.

Dr. Heather Gornik, one of Cleveland Clinic's cardiologists and vascular medicine specialists, is one example. She is one of the few doctors in the country who specialize in treating fibromuscular dysplasia (FMD), a condition marked by narrowing of the blood vessels. She knows a great deal about FMD, but what she *really* knows how to do is listen.

Years ago, when Dr. Gornik was a resident in Boston, she saved a patient's life by listening very closely, using a stethoscope to detect the distinctive murmur of a leaky aortic valve in the heart of a man who was having severe chest pain. In someone with this condition, the heart valve doesn't close properly, allowing blood to leak back across the valve. This patient's leaking aortic valve resulted from a tear in the aorta (aortic dissection), the main blood vessel of the body. The doctors in charge of the case weren't aware of the aortic dissection and were about to give the patient blood thinners for a possible heart attack. Doing so probably would have exacerbated the problem, causing the patient to bleed to death internally. Instead, the patient was properly diagnosed through testing and underwent lifesaving surgery.

These days, Dr. Gornik spends hours at patients' bedsides and in her office listening for the telltale signs of FMD, which she describes as a particular kind of "swooshing." Despite the plethora of sophisticated techniques and equipment available in medicine, sometimes there's nothing better than a stethoscope and an experienced, caring doctor who knows how to listen. Dr. Gornik takes time with her patients, remembering not merely what their heart sounds like but the details of their lives. As she remarked in a newspaper interview, "If you listen, you'll hear things."[24]

Putting patients first is easier for doctors working in a large group practice because they're not distracted by the many tasks required to run a business. They don't have to file their own insurance claims, bill patients, hire employees, or buy supplies and equipment—the larger group takes care of all that. They also don't have to worry about the potentially devastating effect of a malpractice lawsuit, because they are covered by the larger group's malpractice insurance and lawyers. Consequently, they can offer treatments that patients need but that doctors elsewhere might be hesitant to recommend because of the risk.

I did my training in conventional hospitals, where doctors received fees for the services they provided. When I came to Cleveland Clinic, I found it wonderfully liberating because I didn't have to worry about ordering more tests or steering more patients toward a certain kind of surgery. It didn't make a difference to my income what medical decisions I made—I knew at the beginning of the year how much I would earn. I could relax and focus completely on my patients and *their* needs. At the same time, I was driven to excel, because I knew that, like all staff members at Cleveland Clinic, I had only an annual contract, and at the end of the year my performance would be reviewed. I would be expected to have seen a certain number of patients and to have performed a certain number of procedures, but that was only part of what determined whether I stayed, was granted a raise, or was asked to leave. I was held accountable for the *quality* of the care that I provided. To this day, as CEO, I still have only an annual contract, and I am still held accountable for the quality of the work that I do.

Dr. Bradford Borden, who chairs Cleveland Clinic's Emergency Services Institute, agreed that working for a large group practice has numerous benefits: "I used to work in a more conventional medical setting. I wouldn't want to diminish anything that anyone does in a private practice setting, but I do think that having a large group take care of billing and the like gives you the time and ability to focus on being a better professional. I know I've been able to become a better doctor not just technically, but in all other respects— in how I interact with patients, how I evaluate and decide on the course of care, and how I keep up with trends and new treatments."

Although there are excellent doctors practicing everywhere, the working conditions at large group practices allow institutions such as Cleveland Clinic to compete more effectively for the best talent. Our doctors regularly turn down offers to work for other top hospitals for big salary increases; even though the pay is less at Cleveland Clinic, the ability to focus on the patient makes the practice of medicine there more rewarding. Doctors at Cleveland Clinic have more time than they would have elsewhere to keep track of the latest developments in their specialty, to pursue research, and to care for patients who require more of their attention, because they're not bearing the entire economic and administrative burden of running a practice. Only 4 percent of Cleveland Clinic physicians leave each year to practice elsewhere—a significantly lower turnover than the 6.8 percent national average turnover in medical groups in 2012.[25]

Is Higher-Quality Care Affordable?

Healthcare costs nationwide have increased more rapidly than the rest of the economy for 32 of the past 40 years and are expected to become the single biggest slice of the national budget. A quarter of state budgets are spent on Medicaid.[26] Unfortunately, much of this money is wasted because the system isn't functioning optimally. It's like trying to warm an old house in winter when all the windows are open. And just as homeowners can dramatically lower their heating bill by adding insulation, installing double-paned Energy Star windows, and upgrading their furnace to a more energy-efficient model, the nation's healthcare system can similarly lower costs by, among other things, centralizing care and administration, improving patient outcomes, and reducing readmissions.

The potential for group practices to control costs is built into their very structure. Doctors who are paid a salary won't be tempted by the financial incentive to order possibly unnecessary tests and procedures. But that's just the beginning. Just as large groups of doctors can more easily introduce changes to make their practices run more efficiently and economically, they can effectively push through reforms that enhance quality.

Quality Improvement Measures Boost Patient Satisfaction and the Bottom Line

Some quality-enhancing reforms, such as putting more doctors in intensive care units, do cost more money. But a great number of other reforms improve quality *and* decrease cost at the same time. Cleveland Clinic's revamped procedures for treating lung transplant patients—which resulted in 3 percent more patients being alive after 30 days—decreased related costs by 6 percent. When Geisinger improved its coronary artery bypass surgery process to save lives, it reduced the cost for treating each patient by almost 5 percent.[27] By reducing the number of induced births at its facilities and thereby lowering the number of cesarean sections performed, Intermountain saved $50 million. Intermountain estimates that if hospitals everywhere introduced its reforms, the annual savings would be $3.5 billion[28] (yes, *billion*)—and that's for just one procedure.

Good patient care is synonymous with fiscal health. If a group practice isn't sustaining itself with the money it brings in, it can't do very much to help patients over the long term. The issue is not simply a choice between cutting costs with abandon and pampering patients with every last luxury that money can buy; it is balancing cost and quality to achieve *good value*. Cleveland Clinic and other leading large group practices assess the care provided using a fraction, with the numerator being quality of care and the denominator being cost. This paints a total picture that enables a large group practice to be run like a business, serving customers well while adequately funding its operations.

As salaried members of the same organization, doctors at large group practices can introduce comprehensive cultures of improvement, working in real time to cut waste. These cultures of improvement are as sophisticated as those seen in leading corporations around the world—and they're getting results. ThedaCare, a group in northeastern Wisconsin, implemented a process to help its frontline workers solve daily problems and improve the system. Quality soared, patients were more satisfied, and staff members became more engaged in their jobs—even as the group cut costs, giving its finances a substantial boost. Virginia Mason Medical Center in Seattle adapted elements of the same system that Toyota uses to build its cars more efficiently. The change resulted in patients spending more quality time with physicians and there being fewer errors in their care, even as costs decreased and the center remained profitable.[29]

Care Paths Help Ensure Uniform Treatment and Lower Costs

Over the past several years, Cleveland Clinic and other progressive institutions have begun to systematically review the care they provide and to develop standard care paths for treating patients. This process involves studying, deconstructing, and charting every stage of treatment, from the moment the patient comes in to the moment he leaves the hospital. Quality and cost come under consideration. Clear processes are established to coordinate the services of doctors, nurses, and other caregivers. Guidelines are established for when to order tests, when to consider surgery, and other clinical decisions.

Because one of the goals of care paths is to reduce costs, assigning business managers to oversee the efficiency side of care path development is tempting. But Cleveland Clinic has assembled an interdisciplinary group of doctors and other caregivers to provide oversight. These people are all on salary. They're all on the same team. What at another institution might turn into battles over turf and resources plays out at Cleveland Clinic as negotiation and compromise. Clinical policies that affect the quality of patient care can be rolled out across Cleveland Clinic's system of hospitals without the fear of pushback from entrenched interests. And a patient receives the same quality of care at any of our facilities.

One example is Cleveland Clinic's approach to developing a care path for hip and knee replacement surgeries. These are extremely common procedures, usually done to ease the symptoms of arthritis. Traditionally, a patient would come in with a badly arthritic knee, and a doctor would refer him to an orthopedic surgeon. The surgeon might schedule the patient for surgery without saying too much to the patient about what to expect or when she might be released. Every surgeon and primary care physician might have a slightly different process for handling his portion of the care that the patient receives. To the patient, the process might seem chaotic and haphazard. Important parts of the care might fall through the cracks. The anesthesiologist might not know the nuances of the patient's medical condition, or the time allotted for postoperative recovery might not be sufficient. The surgery might go well, but the patient might go home less than satisfied with her experience. Care paths are intended to minimize these variations and ensure that each patient is provided with the highest-quality care.

In redesigning the joint replacement care path, the Cleveland Clinic team began its research by talking with primary care physicians because they manage arthritis nonsurgically. Discussions centered on developing the best timetable for referring patients for surgery to ensure that surgery is done at the time and place where it will most benefit each patient and be most cost-effective for the organization. The team also contemplated how Cleveland Clinic could help primary care physicians better prepare patients for surgery, coordinate with other specialists (such as endocrinologists if patients are diabetic), and ensure that patients see the right care providers before surgery (such as anesthesiologists to discuss special needs and anxieties). After surgery, the care path involves rehabilitation specialists to assist with patients' recovery. All these steps minimize the risk of infection and other complications—improving patients' outcomes while reducing costs. The utility of this care path is clear: it's allowing Cleveland Clinic to offer better hip and knee surgeries at a lower price.[30]

Dr. Mark Froimson, who has overseen the creation of Cleveland Clinic's care path effort, believes that the group practice model has been integral to the development of relevant and effective care paths. He said, "Think about it. You're redesigning a whole episode of care that affects many different physicians. In another system, competing interests might hamper an effort like this. However, because we all work within the same system and have shared incentives, because we don't work in silos, we're freed up to rethink the care we give the patient and to do it quickly. We can coordinate everyone involved more efficiently and provide Medicare with one low price. We also measure how well patients do to make sure that the care path we designed works the way we hoped it would."

Care paths—and the kind of organizational focus that enables their development—are part of the exciting future of medicine. As Dr. Froimson noted, "What's remarkable in medicine is that we've been giving patients a one-way ticket into the hospital without outlining in any carefully planned way what's going to happen and when they're going home. Now we're doing that, and of course if you can plan something out in advance, you can do it more efficiently and save money. You can also do it smartly, in a way that helps you have the very best experience."

Bundled Healthcare Services Provide Value to Large Companies

Because Cleveland Clinic can design care paths so effectively, seamlessly bringing together a large number of relevant providers and specialties, it can calculate a single price—a "bundle"—for a hip or knee replacement operation and offer it to Medicare at a discount. Cleveland Clinic has done this at one of its hospitals, developing a care path that gets patients out of the hospital and recovering faster while saving Medicare an average of about 3 percent per joint replacement patient.

Beyond developing care paths, the sheer size of large group practices enables them to deliver high-quality care much more efficiently. Thus, they can negotiate with big companies to provide them with discounts on common procedures that their employees may need. This approach is often called a "bundled payment" program. For example, Cleveland Clinic has a contract with the retailer Lowe's for the heart surgeries its employees undergo. Because Cleveland Clinic knows that it will be handling a certain amount of Lowe's business, it can organize its staff more efficiently and give Lowe's a good bulk price. It's actually *cheaper* for Lowe's to fly its employees from around the country to Cleveland for heart surgery because Lowe's knows in advance exactly what the procedure will cost. The company also knows that Cleveland Clinic's cardiac surgical outcomes are the best in the country, so despite its savings, it is not scrimping on the quality of care. In some cases, Cleveland Clinic cardiologists have determined that patients sent by Lowe's don't really need surgery and can be treated with medicine or some less invasive procedure. Again, because all Cleveland Clinic doctors are salaried, they have no financial incentive to order unnecessary treatment. The goal is simply to give each patient the best care—an orientation that saves a large company such as Lowe's even more money.

Walmart was a pioneer of bundled payments, as one might expect from a company that built a reputation on finding ways to cut expenses and pass the savings on to consumers. The Walmart program allows associates to receive necessary heart, spine, and transplant surgeries at Cleveland Clinic, Mayo Clinic, Geisinger Medical Center, Mercy Hospital Springfield, Scott & White Memorial Hospital, or Virginia Mason Medical Center with no out-of-pocket costs. These hospitals were chosen, according to Walmart, because they met "the highest quality standards for heart, spine and transplant surgery." Clearly, these providers also represent a broad geographic spread. The program began in 1996 as a partnership with Mayo Clinic to cover transplants. Walmart executives were pleased by the fact that Mayo Clinic doctors didn't immediately perform an expensive transplant on every Walmart associate referred there but first pursued other, less costly options.[31]

Large Groups Have More Purchasing Power

Hospitals use hundreds of billions of dollars' worth of supplies every year. Medical supplies can be exorbitantly expensive: a single suture can cost $500 or more.

In a conventional hospital, any number of small groups representing different medical specialties might order their own supplies, paying higher prices because they're not buying in volume. The size of large group practices translates into more purchasing power, greater leverage in negotiations, and better prices associated with buying in bulk.

Cleveland Clinic not only negotiates better deals with its suppliers, but also systematically evaluates its operations to see where it is wasting money. A large team of doctors and other specialists analyzed the outcomes of specific surgical procedures and the supplies used during those procedures, looking for ways the organization might achieve the same or better results at less cost. For example, the team inventoried all the supplies—from the laboratory, the nurses' station, the surgical supply room, and so on—used during a prostatectomy (surgical removal of the prostate). The team identified every test, every suture, and every piece of equipment in the operating room. Invariably, looking at a complex medical procedure that closely will reveal costs that are often taken for granted but are in fact wasteful and contribute nothing of value to the patient outcome—everything from the cost of sutures to processes in the labs. Cutting these unnecessary expenses resulted in a 15 percent cost savings in the first year and 25 percent after two years—without compromising patient outcomes.

Because the best doctors and hospitals are so focused on patients' needs, they don't always weigh the costs and benefits of the supplies and instruments that they use. Asking them to be mindful of the advantages and disadvantages of the tools they use every day can lead to some remarkable discoveries. For example, Cleveland Clinic's liver transplant surgeons typically used one of two kinds of staplers to reattach blood vessels and stop bleeding. One model cost $4,000, and the other cost $1,400. When asked which model they preferred, the surgeons didn't particularly favor one over the other. Once they were compelled to think about it, they collectively asked themselves: "Why do we even use staplers? We can just as safely and easily stop the bleeding using sutures that cost only $5 apiece. Why don't we stop using staplers altogether?" It was a simple fix that cut costs.

This kind of analysis requires practice group administrators to consider the following questions and responses:

- Are we performing the procedure in the same way as other leading institutions? If not, why not?

- If something we're doing costs more, are we providing more value for the patient for the increased cost? If not, we need to change what we're doing.

- Is there something we *should* be doing for patients, even if it costs a little more in the short term?

Cleveland Clinic Case Study

At Cleveland Clinic, we encourage different areas of the organization to perform the kind of analysis just described by holding them accountable for saving money. In 2009, Cleveland Clinic set an organizational goal of reducing the amount it was spending on supplies of various kinds. It took its inspiration from Apple, a company that maintains stringent control over the cost of supplies. To help the internal cost-cutting committees, we set out to raise care providers' consciousness, putting price tags on instruments and supplies and posting the costs of supplies where caregivers could see them. The goal was to make caregivers mindful about supply use. These efforts helped the organization reach its goal of cutting spending on supplies by $100 million over two years.

To promote ongoing cost awareness and savings, we created scorecards that quantify and measure quality and cost, and we set goals: "Cut your costs on heart valve implants by 20 percent while improving quality by 10 percent." We check the progress on these scorecards every three months. If we don't see movement in the right direction, we ask new questions and implement ways to encourage and reward cost-saving measures.

Adopting this approach in a conventional setting would be difficult because the doctors all work for different organizations with different bottom lines. In a group practice, it's considerably easier. Dr. Robert Wyllie, chief medical operations officer, explained, "It's easier to gain consensus when everyone is on the same page and looking at the same strategic goals and vision"—something that can happen only when everyone is receiving a salary from the same source.

Implications for Healthcare Consumers

Large group practices are the face of *real* healthcare reform, but unfortunately, this is something that often gets lost in the heat of political debate. Group practices just work better, for a host of reasons, and that's why they are starting to pick up steam nationally.

What does this mean for healthcare consumers? Those who have one or more large group practices in their area should compare them with one another and with independent practices to assess the quality and affordability of the care they provide.[32] Those who live in a place without a large group practice can ask their doctors directly what they are doing to improve the quality of the care they provide. They can inquire whether the practice or the hospital where the doctor operates routinely reviews how it treats patients to get the best results. A patient who doesn't understand why a doctor is ordering a particular test should ask whether that test is really necessary. Most often it will be, but alternatives might exist.

Large group practices are already revolutionizing American medicine. This is progress that affects all healthcare consumers directly, even if it might not seem so at first blush. When more and more doctors organize themselves more effectively, when they come together and run hospitals like large innovative companies, everyone wins.

Collaborative Care Is More Effective

S tephanie Zimmerman was eight years old when she was diagnosed with Ewing's sarcoma, a rare childhood bone cancer that required aggressive treatment. The experience inspired Stephanie to pursue a career as an oncology nurse-practitioner, but it also wreaked havoc on her heart.

In her thirties, Stephanie discovered that the lifesaving chemotherapy and radiation treatment that she'd received as a child had damaged her heart tissue. The potential consequences were unknown. Although she and her husband, John, were aware that having a damaged heart intensified the ordinary risks of childbirth, they welcomed their son, Abel, into the world. Over the years, Stephanie felt that something was changing—she was experiencing fatigue at a new level. Her doctors found that her heart was not pumping efficiently. Too little oxygen-bearing blood was getting to her tissues.

When Stephanie was 38, her heart began to show signs of failing. She traveled from her hometown of Atlanta to Cleveland Clinic to have two of her heart valves repaired. The surgery was successful and relieved her symptoms. A few months later, however, her symptoms reappeared: intolerable fatigue, shortness of breath, and fluid retention. The damage to her heart had gone deeper than the valves. "The surgery had unmasked the fact that the chemotherapy drug I had as a child did damage to the left ventricular muscle," Stephanie recounted. "Once the valves were repaired, the damaged left ventricle could not handle the extra pressure, and I spiraled into heart failure."

After three months, her heart function had worsened, and she learned that if she did not get a new heart, she would die. A local hospital turned her down for a transplant, considering it too risky based on her complex medical history and recent surgery. Cleveland Clinic accepted her as a candidate for transplant, and two months later she was airlifted to the hospital with end-stage heart failure.

Dr. Randall Starling, section head of heart failure and cardiac transplant medicine at Cleveland Clinic, was on call when Stephanie arrived. He informed the family that she might live only a few hours and had to go on the transplant list immediately. Twelve hours later, they found a heart that was a perfect match. Cardiothoracic surgeon Dr. Nicholas Smedira performed the successful transplant surgery, which took nearly 12 hours. "When I woke up," Stephanie recalled, "I could feel the heartbeat, and it was so strong. Before the transplant, I couldn't feel my heart beating because it was so weak and inefficient."

Because of her compromised immune system, doctors had to keep Stephanie intubated for 42 days. Four large teams took care of her for more than a year, including heart, kidney, lung, and intensive care unit doctors, infection specialists, and a support staff of nurses, technicians, and physical therapists. There were hundreds of people in total.

"My team was huge," Stephanie said. "I watched them working and felt like something supernatural was taking place. I'd never seen people work together so well like that. Communication was seamless; everyone who saw me knew what the other specialists and team members were doing and what their goals were. Nobody on the team had an ego." Stephanie especially appreciated the efforts her team made to accommodate four-year-old Abel and her husband, who was trying to continue with his job remotely.

Stephanie spent 12 weeks at Cleveland Clinic. As of 2013, she and her family are doing well. Stephanie credited the daily support and encouragement provided by her medical team for her recovery. "I've just never seen a multidisciplinary team wage a sustained campaign like that and perform at such a high level. This group of professionals was consistently 'in the zone.' I don't know how they did it."

The Power of Collaboration

Coordinating business processes such as the payment of salaries, purchasing of supplies, billing, and organizational improvement is a key advantage of large group practices in that it frees up physicians to concentrate on providing better patient care. But improved patient outcomes result from more than just administrative efficiency—they stem from taking a team approach to the clinical treatment of patients like Stephanie Zimmerman. Increased collaboration among medical disciplines is visible today across the American healthcare system, and many medical authorities laud its merits. Yet collaboration is advancing with special force in large, physician-run group practices such as Cleveland Clinic. In these practices, collaboration is streamlining care and saving lives.

It's easy to see why better teamwork can improve medical treatment. Medical knowledge today is vast—approximately 1,500 medical articles appear *each day* in about 4,000 journals.[1] Individual physicians can master only small portions of a patient's care. When patients get sick, they typically have to visit numerous specialists to get proper treatment. One study found that between 2000 and 2002, the typical Medicare beneficiary with a chronic condition such as diabetes or heart disease saw up to 16 physicians in the course of a year, not to mention pharmacists, imaging technicians, and other specialists.[2]

Collaboration becomes more important as illnesses or conditions become more complex. To treat a patient who is experiencing epileptic seizures, for example, a neurologist will usually provide medication. If the seizures continue, scans are done, and a doctor who specializes in imaging the brain helps read the images to find out where in the brain the seizures originate. A neuropsychologist assesses the precise effects that the disease is having on a person's functioning, given that surgical procedures can help improve some areas of function (such as memory) more than others. If surgery is indicated, a highly specialized neurosurgeon will perform the operation.

All in all, effective treatment of epilepsy, a disease affecting 1 to 2 percent of the population, might require coordinating a half dozen or more specialists—in addition to nurses and technicians—to provide the best care. If these professionals work together as a tight-knit team, patients receive treatments that reflect the perspectives of a number of specialists, not just one or two. The handoff between specialists becomes more fluid, inconveniencing patients less and resulting in fewer mistakes. Doctors educate one another about the case, enabling each to understand the patient more deeply and make better recommendations. The wasteful duplication of tests and scans is minimized. That is only the beginning of the list of benefits.

Studies show a need for better transitions between specialties and a perception by many doctors that better coordination is required.[3] The good news is that change is coming. Doctors are reorganizing themselves to increase collaboration in dealing with specific patients and their illnesses, and this collaboration is helping to produce breakthrough innovations in care.

The Teamwork Incubator

In the early twentieth century, when physicians first came together to form group practices such as Mayo Clinic and Cleveland Clinic, their purpose was to bring doctors together not just organizationally but *clinically*. The medical profession had already classified doctors by specialties, starting with medieval guilds that distinguished between medical doctors and surgeons and intensifying with the emergence of modern medical and surgical specialization during the nineteenth century. Almost 100 years ago, the founders of group practices were struck by the complexity of modern medicine and the consequent need for collaboration across specialties. Cleveland Clinic founder Dr. George Crile observed that a modern-day doctor is no more able to undertake intricate patient problems alone than to build a car alone.[4]

Dr. Crile and his colleagues envisaged their ideal medical center as a kind of teamwork incubator, a place where a variety of perspectives, including cutting-edge laboratory science, would be brought to bear on a patient's malady. In Crile's words, "We have . . . created an organization . . . to the end that in making a diagnosis or planning a treatment, the clinician may have at his disposal the advantages of the laboratories of the applied sciences and of colleagues with special training in the various branches of medicine and surgery."[5] On the occasion of Cleveland Clinic's opening, Dr. William J. Mayo of Mayo Clinic likewise described how in this new group practice, "the internist, the surgeon, and the specialist may join with the physiologist, the pathologist, and the laboratory workers to form the clinical group, which must also include men learned in the abstract sciences."[6]

Drs. Crile and Mayo weren't out to subvert the individual doctor's autonomy. They sought to empower doctors by gathering them into large units composed of mutually supportive colleagues. They knew that this worked because they'd seen it during World

War I, when doctors from many specialties collaborated to restore the wounded to health.

The selflessness that often characterizes the military can be seen in the group practice, in which credit is shared and pay and volume are decoupled. As Dr. Smedira, the surgeon who operated on Stephanie Zimmerman, said, "Nobody here is given incentives to push his or her own services. I'm paid the same whether I do a surgery myself or hand it off to a more suitable colleague. I can look at the case from the patient's perspective and not think in the back of my mind about needing to fill my schedule."

Over the years, Cleveland Clinic's group practice has built a rich culture of community and teamwork. The system selects for collaborative personalities, such as the chief of staff, Dr. Joseph Hahn, a neurosurgeon who skillfully manages the professional lives of 3,000 doctors and scientists in 120 specialties and subspecialties. He came to Cleveland Clinic from the Philadelphia area purely to pick up some training and then go home. But the collaborative spirit made him want to stay. "I so much enjoyed the way people worked together that I was never tempted to leave," he said. "This whole approach of team spirit and helping each other out is so special."

On one of his first days at Cleveland Clinic, Dr. Hahn was in the operating room when a plastic surgeon working in the room next door came in looking for help. The plastic surgeon explained that he was in the middle of reshaping a patient's skull and had run into a neurological complication that he couldn't solve by himself. "That made an impression on me. I didn't say, 'What did you do? How could you be so stupid?' I just went in and fixed the problem and went on with my day. That's the way it was here then; that's the way it *still* is."

The physicians at Cleveland Clinic don't wait for collaborative problem solving to arise by happenstance—they've created an organization in which it happens every day. Steve Jobs said, "Innovation comes from people meeting up in the hallways or calling each other at 10:30 at night." At Cleveland Clinic, the facilities are designed to maximize serendipitous encounters among caregivers. The busy lobbies and skyways are the scenes of many a "curbside consultation" and impromptu brainstorming session. A two-block-long skyway connects the outpatient and inpatient facilities. Throughout the day, people in white coats move across the skyway, passing back and forth between offices, examination rooms, laboratories, and hospital rooms. Medical conventions and continuing education sessions from the connected hotel and conference center spill into this area as well, adding visitors and outside physicians to the milieu.

For an example of what can happen when doctors in various specialties come together like this in one institution, consider the response of Cleveland Clinic's digestive disease specialists to the little-known but serious problem known as pouchitis. This condition affects patients who have had their bowel removed as a treatment for ulcerative colitis, colon cancer, or some other bowel condition, and replaced by a kind of pouch that is surgically fashioned out of intestinal tissue. The pouch is an alternative to having to wear an external bag to collect waste; it represents a major improvement in quality of life for patients who have it. The trade-off is that about 10 years after surgery, some patients develop inflammation of the pouch, called pouchitis, or some other pouch disorder. These disorders are difficult to diagnose and treat. Because the pouch procedure has been performed only since the 1980s, these problems are relatively new.

By 2002, the incidence of pouchitis was rising quickly with the increasing use of the pouch procedure worldwide, yet no specialized center was available to address it. That year, colorectal surgeons at Cleveland Clinic created the world's first multidisciplinary Pouchitis Clinic, which has become a national and international referral center for pouchitis and related disorders. The clinic is staffed by a team of Cleveland Clinic adult and pediatric gastroenterologists, colorectal surgeons, gastrointestinal pathologists, gastrointestinal radiologists, basic scientists, and biostatisticians. It specializes in the surgical construction of the pouch and the reconstruction of failed pouches, along with medical and endoscopic management of pouchitis and related disorders.

In its first year, the Pouchitis Clinic saw 60 patients; today, it treats more than 1,000 a year. Of these, 65 percent come from outside Ohio and from around the world, testifying to the extent of the unmet need. It is difficult to imagine an innovative niche center like this being organized, launched, and scaled up to this level with such ease outside a nonprofit, multispecialty group practice. It is also difficult to imagine it originating in an organizational culture that does not emphasize regular and informal cross-disciplinary collaboration.

Pushing Medicine Further Through Multispecialty Collaboration

The clinical effects of countless daily casual encounters and informal consultations have yet to be quantified. Still, such interactions are vital to the care of patients at large group practices. One of the most powerful benefits of multispecialty collaboration is the confidence that doctors feel when they take on extremely sick, frail, or elderly patients whose risk profiles might ordinarily exclude them from potentially lifesaving treatments. The source of this confidence is the knowledge that a top-notch specialist is always on hand to treat whatever surprises or complications may occur.

Surgical complication rates at the top hospitals aren't much different from those at the lowest-ranking hospitals.[7] What sets the two apart is the doctors' ability to rescue patients once complications occur. The best hospitals have stronger teams, with physicians and others who are all-stars in their specialties. Being the best isn't merely about being multidisciplinary but also about having the right players with the ability and the desire to work together. Doctors who have a strong team behind them feel more comfortable pushing the envelope on what they know is possible. That's what happened in the case of Stephanie Zimmerman, the patient whose story we told at the beginning of this chapter.

In caring for the sickest patients, teamwork enables doctors in large group practices to go beyond existing treatments and pioneer new ones. For example, in one challenging form of kidney cancer, long, slender tumors can snake up the inferior vena cava (the large blood vessel that carries blood from all over the body into the heart) and threaten to block blood flow. In cases that I helped treat during the 1980s, a urological surgeon would mobilize the kidney and prepare it for removal while I, a thoracic and cardiovascular surgeon, would stop the patient's heart and redirect the blood flow to a heart-lung machine before extricating the tumor from the blood vessel. Unfortunately, the operation could take longer than it is advisable to keep a patient on the heart-lung machine, so we needed some other way to reduce blood flow to the vena cava. Together, we came up with the idea of arresting patients' circulation by deep hypothermia, or extreme cold. Once the patients were cooled down, we had more time to remove the tumor and the kidney, and then we warmed them up again following the operation. Using hypothermia is now a standard part of the procedure for treating certain renal cancers involving the inferior vena cava.

There is a natural gulf between specialties such as thoracic and cardiovascular surgery and urological surgery, but this example is one of hundreds that demonstrate how frictionless multispecialty collaboration has solved complex medical problems and has extended life for many seriously ill patients. True creativity in medicine doesn't take place within disciplines so much as it does *at the boundaries between disciplines.* Increasing opportunities for collaboration among specialists and instilling a culture that encourages creativity will lead to the creation of exciting new treatments that save lives.

As another example of the power of collaborative medicine, I was part of a group of thoracic and cardiovascular surgeons that recognized the need for a device that would control patients' blood pressure after cardiac surgery. Postsurgical high blood pressure is a serious problem that can lead to numerous complications, from disruption of vascular suture lines to stroke. The standard practice was to have a nurse assess patients' needs and administer the appropriate dose of sodium nitroprusside to lower the blood pressure.

Recognizing the need for this to be done automatically, we called on a biomedical engineer from Cleveland Clinic's Lerner Research Institute to help construct and program a device to monitor patients' blood pressure and deliver the medication as needed. We published our discovery in 1989.[8]

The nature of the multispecialty group practice removed many of the barriers that might have inhibited our three-year collaboration on the device—a collaboration that led to a patent and the launch of a new product for patient care.

Hybrid Operating Rooms Maximize Collaboration

If there's one place in the modern hospital that embodies collaboration at the leading edge of healthcare, it's the hybrid operating room. Such a room is equipped to perform both minimally invasive, catheter-based procedures and conventional open surgery—sometimes simultaneously. More and more medical centers are building and equipping hybrid rooms that can be used for cardiovascular, neurological, orthopedic, and other procedures. As of 2013, Cleveland Clinic has two and is soon to have four hybrid rooms in its Thoracic and Cardiovascular Surgery area.

The hybrid operating rooms have powerful imaging capabilities, including 3D CT, MRI, and x-ray machines that deliver detailed pictures from inside the body during a procedure. A giant robotic C-arm dominates the room. This device resembles the robots developed for automobile assembly lines, and it's capable of a wide range of movements. At first glance, the hybrid operating room looks like the command deck of a science-fiction starship, with a glassed-in control room, glowing screens, monitors, and an eerily mobile robotic arm. Every specialized piece of equipment is designed to facilitate the next generation of minimally invasive and open surgery.

Among the procedures done in this room are new treatments to prevent the deadly rupture of aortic aneurysms. The "gold standard" treatment for a dangerously distended aortic aneurysm is open surgery. The team needs to stop the heart and redirect the circulation to a mechanical heart-lung device before opening the patient (as one doctor described it) "from stem to stern." Whole portions of the diseased aorta are cut away and replaced with a stent (synthetic fiber tubing) before blood flow is restored, the patient is revived, and the long recovery begins.

Today, surgeons, cardiologists, and radiologists are collaborating on a new way to repair aortic aneurysms that eliminates the need to stop the heart and make a huge incision. A light, wire-framed cloth tube anywhere from 1 to 3 inches long (a stent graft) is collapsed to the width of a cocktail straw and slipped into the blood vessel at the tip of a wirelike catheter. Doctors watching real-time x-ray images guide the wire and its tiny cargo through the blood vessels. When the stent graft reaches the spot where the aorta is either ballooning dangerously or falling apart, the doctors pull a kind of trigger that expands the tube against the inside walls of the blood vessel. Then the delivery catheter is withdrawn, and the expanded tube becomes the blood vessel's new interior conduit.

The aorta is a long blood vessel with many complexities. It branches; it meanders; it varies in configuration from individual to individual. Aneurysms can occur in narrow, twisting, or branched segments of the aorta that are hard to reach. Cleveland Clinic innovators have pioneered the development and placement of stents for these awkward places.

The hybrid room is a model of systems integration, combining human eyes, high-tech imaging, and advanced surgical technology and support.

What kind of caregivers thrive in a hybrid operating room? Hybrid doctors—those who practice more than one specialty.

Dr. Eric Roselli is a Cleveland Clinic cardiac surgeon who is trained in the minimally invasive techniques that interventional cardiologists perform. He is currently working on a new technique that would make open surgery unnecessary for elderly people. Often, patients have been rejected for open aortic arch repair because they were too sick or frail. Dr. Roselli's technique relies on a method called "rapid pacing" to temporarily disrupt the patient's normal heart function and blood flow, then delivers a stent graft to the aortic arch through an incision in the bottom of the heart.

To develop this procedure, Dr. Roselli combined a number of techniques he had learned in interventional cardiology, endovascular surgery, and conventional heart surgery—long-established treatments that had never been combined in quite this way. He credits this cross-disciplinary learning to the collaborative environment in which he works. "It has been easy for me here to spend time with my colleagues over in cardiovascular medicine and thoracic and cardiovascular surgery so that they could teach me the catheter skills I needed, which they use every day to treat aortic disease."

Dr. Roselli moved among cardiac catheterization labs, operating rooms, and the hybrid rooms while he was developing his procedure. "I was learning from other specialties without pushback. Nobody said I was stepping into his or her territory or thought I was trying to take patients away. Their response was, 'Sure, Eric, what would you like me to teach you?'" All the cardiovascular specialties at Cleveland Clinic have a long history of collaborating. Dr. Roselli was able to reap the benefits of that collaboration, taking insights from multiple disciplines and treating patients in ways that few others in the world had done.

Working Together in Institutes

When it comes to caring for patients, location matters, and grouping physicians around diseases matters too. Traditionally, doctors haven't grouped themselves this way. They've separated themselves into departments that correspond to their specialties: Department of Dermatology, Department of Cardiology, Department of Pediatrics. Typically, these departments are divided further into medical subspecialties. But patients don't experience their illness or condition in terms of academic departments or divisions. Patients who have a complex condition such as diabetes or a brain tumor often require the expertise of many different specialists. Traditionally, that has required them to move among various departments to get care, often going from building to building on a medical campus and having to navigate the different cultures, norms, and billing processes of each specialty. It has meant that some of the doctors involved in their care weren't communicating with other doctors as fully as possible, leading to duplicate tests. Also, because some departments are more profitable than others, patients often have had to contend with understaffing and underfunding in the less profitable departments (such as psychology) relative to the more profitable ones (such as heart surgery).

The next phase of physician collaboration—one that's actually been in the works since the 1990s—will involve the creation at many medical centers of larger, full-fledged institutes focused on specific diseases or organ systems. Michael Porter, a healthcare expert from Harvard University, has written: "Our system of uncoordinated, sequential visits to multiple providers, physicians, departments and specialties works against value. Instead we need to move to integrated practice units that encompass all the skills and services required over the full cycle of care for each medical condition."[9]

Disease-oriented institutes allow patients to get the care they need in one place, without traveling between geographically separate departments. They also greatly facilitate the casual physical interaction of medical specialists, allowing patients to get the very best care for their complex ailments. In addition, integrating low-profit and high-profit specialties into one unit with one bottom line enables the high-profit specialties to pay for the low-profit portions, thus making both fully accessible to the patients who need them. Most fundamentally, the institute is a vital expression of the philosophy of "putting patients first." As Porter has argued, "A medical condition should be defined from the patient's perspective. It should encompass the set of illnesses or injuries that are best addressed with a dedicated and integrated care delivery model."[10] That's precisely the kind of thinking that's embodied in the disease-focused institute.

Cleveland Clinic has pushed the institute model further than any other organization. In 2008, it did away with departments as the primary organizing unit across the entire organization and replaced them with 27 clinical, research, educational, and support institutes. This change was based on the belief that patients would benefit from improved communication among personnel, billing, and access to and geographic clustering of the services they'd need. In addition, a multidisciplinary approach would guide diagnostic and therapeutic decisions while facilitating the launching of educational programs and encouraging scientific inquiry. Further, disease-focused institutes that used standardized ways of measuring outcomes and other variables would help Cleveland Clinic better determine how well and how efficiently it was treating diseases.

The institute structure fundamentally changed the organizational relationships among thousands of physicians. Many of them arrived at work one morning to find that they had new supervisors and new coworkers in an organizational unit that hadn't existed the day before. Even so, staff members offered few objections. They clearly understood the potential that institutes had to enhance patient care. Having everyone on the same team allowed the organization to envisage institutes, plan them, communicate the change, implement the change, and fine-tune the concept, all without consulting outside interests or cozening internal lobbies.

The forces that might have been aligned against this change are powerful—forces such as inertia and the temptation to continue doing things the way they've always been done. Some people might have argued that Cleveland Clinic was already one of the most successful hospitals in the world, so if it wasn't broken, why fix it? But as hockey player Wayne Gretzky famously pointed out, success comes not from being where the puck is at the moment but from skating to where it's going. Despite the fact that Cleveland Clinic was already highly successful, it needed to be ready for where healthcare was going to be years down the line. Now, at the beginning of the future it was preparing for, Cleveland Clinic is well positioned.

An examination of the evolution of Cleveland Clinic's Glickman Urological & Kidney Institute may provide a sense of how the institute model has improved collaboration and enhanced patient care. In 2007, the Department of Urology wasn't "broken." It was the largest and most specialized urology practice in the world and was ranked number two in America by *U.S. News & World Report*. Urology is a surgical specialty that deals with the urinary system and reproductive organs. Its medical counterpart is nephrology, which provides nonsurgical treatment for diseases and disorders of the kidneys (including high blood pressure, a condition that originates in the kidneys).

Because the bladder, kidneys, urinary organs, and sex organs operate as a bundle, the departments of urology and nephrology should work together. That's why Cleveland Clinic combined these two specialties in one institute and linked them with specialists from Cleveland Clinic's Taussig Cancer Institute, Imaging Institute, Ob/Gyn & Women's Health Institute, and others. Patients who are suffering from prostate cancer, kidney cancer, urinary incontinence, sexual issues, and many other urological and kidney-related conditions can now walk into one building and have access to every specialist they need to treat their condition. The doctors who work in the building and nearby can collaborate on leading-edge treatments with fewer physical and institutional barriers than might be found elsewhere.

A good example is the institute's approach to bladder cancer, a potentially life-threatening condition. Less serious cases can be treated with chemotherapy, which is usually delivered intravenously during a number of office visits over the course of several weeks or months. In the past, more serious cases of bladder cancer simply called for the complete surgical removal of the bladder. That protocol changed when new clinical research showed that administering chemotherapy before and after bladder removal reduces the risk that the cancer will return. Now, the clinical oncologists who oversee chemotherapy at Cleveland Clinic work closely with urological surgeons to ensure that patients get the right drug in the right dosage and that treatment begins on the optimal dates before and after surgery. Despite the gulf that normally exists between surgeons and oncologists, Cleveland Clinic's experts in these areas work in concert for the good of the patient.

Another example of a patient-centered outcome stemming from the institute structure is the changes that Cleveland Clinic made in how it treats kidney cancer. In many previous cases, when a patient presented with a large tumor, surgeons removed the entire kidney. The problem was that removing one of a patient's two kidneys could compromise kidney function so much that the patient needed to be on a dialysis machine for the rest of her life. Then the doctors learned of a new class of drug called tyrosine kinase inhibitors, or TKIs, that could help shrink kidney tumors. Using TKIs, the doctors could remove a smaller portion of the kidney, allowing the patient's kidney function to remain intact. The Urological & Kidney Institute introduced a collaborative program for treating patients whose tumors seemed susceptible to downsizing, in which a medical oncologist oversees the administration of the drugs and coordinates with a surgeon who performs the now less major surgery. Throughout the process, the two specialists talk with each other, compare notes, and strategize about the best way for both of them to treat the patient.

Treatment for prostate cancer, a disease that affects millions of men, affords a third example. The various treatments include watchful waiting, radiation, freezing of the prostate gland, brachytherapy, and surgical removal of the prostate. Brachytherapy is the implantation of small radioactive seeds, each the size of a grain of rice, in the prostate. The number of pellets implanted (up to 200) depends on the size and location of the cancer. The implant procedure takes about an hour and is done on an outpatient basis. Although the pellets deliver a higher dose of radiation than conventional treatments that target the prostate with a beam of radiation, the radiation travels only a few millimeters and therefore doesn't affect healthy tissue outside the prostate.

At the Urological & Kidney Institute, every patient who is treated with brachytherapy consults with a radiation therapist and a urologist, who plan the therapy. In the operating room, a urologist, a radiation therapist, and a physicist perform the procedure together. The urologist takes images of the prostate with a sophisticated ultrasound machine. The physicist calculates the exact dose of the seeds used—how many go into the prostate and where they are placed. The radiation therapist places the seeds in the prostate and ensures that the necessary precautions for dealing with radioactive material are taken. As of 2013, institute caregivers have performed this procedure on almost 4,000 patients over 17 years.

Brachytherapy is available at many leading medical centers, but at the Urological & Kidney Institute, the coordination among the various specialists is seamless. The doctors aren't thinking about what share of the revenue from a given procedure is theirs. They don't attempt, even subconsciously, to maintain "control" over the patient in order to maximize revenue. The revenue goes into one pot, one budget. The doctors are thinking only about their patients and the best way to provide treatment using the tools and expertise at their disposal.

The unification of disciplines within the Urological & Kidney Institute also generates useful research, some of which is made possible by the institute's high volume of patients and careful record keeping. For instance, one of the challenges in treating prostate cancer is that some cancers are slow-growing and usually not fatal, whereas others are aggressive, and differentiating the two has been difficult in many cases. Many men have undergone serious treatments and suffered substantial side effects (such as incontinence or impotence), even though their form of prostate cancer probably would never have caused them serious harm. What doctors needed was a reliable biological tool that could assess the severity of the cancer at the time of diagnosis so that they could determine whether to recommend treatment or regular surveillance.

Since the 1990s, Cleveland Clinic has kept a database and tissue bank for the nearly 15,000 patients treated there for prostate cancer. Using those resources, doctors went back to the original tissue biopsies, assessed the gene expression in the tissue on a molecular level, and compared it with the clinical results. This research was interdisciplinary: urologists maintained the database and took the tissue samples, and external scientists performed the analysis. Their joint efforts led to the creation of the first genetic test that allows doctors to biopsy a suspicious prostate and determine—based on a few millimeters of cancer cells—how aggressive the cancer is. This newly available test (slated for market launch as of this writing) will dramatically improve the treatment of prostate cancer and, by making the decision about which treatment to pursue easier, ideally diminish the anxiety that comes with a prostate cancer diagnosis.

Combining urology, urological surgery, and nephrology in the same building under a single leadership was a big move—one that has resulted in a better patient experience, improved lines of internal communication, more integrated clinical services, and more educational and research opportunities for doctors and students. It also boosted the organization's national reputation in these areas. Five years after the change, Cleveland Clinic was ranked number one in America for both urology and kidney disease by *U.S. News & World Report*—both for the first time.[11]

Creating Care Paths:
The Neurological Institute

A care path defines the standard of care for a specific disease or condition from start to finish, beginning with the clinical workflow and including resources, venues, encounters, orders, documentation, results, process, outcome measures, and reports. Putting together a care path for a complex disease or condition requires the involvement of doctors, nurses, administrators, and support personnel at all levels and in multiple specialties. Having all those entities on the same team, under the same leadership, and in the same general area greatly facilitates care path development.

The development of a care path for epilepsy at Cleveland Clinic is a good example. Epilepsy is a brain disorder characterized by episodic seizures, sensory changes, unconsciousness, and other symptoms. It can often be controlled with medication, but sometimes it can't. Cleveland Clinic's Epilepsy Center (overseen by the Neurological Institute) offers patients with epilepsy a range of diagnostic and treatment options based on care paths that it has developed and refined since 2007. Patients who arrive at the center go directly into the care of psychologists and psychiatrists, neurosurgeons, neurologists, and imaging specialists who work as a team to address every aspect of the disease and its ramifications for patients. Each of these specialists contributes a unique perspective:

> *Neurologists* make or confirm the diagnosis of epilepsy, determine the effectiveness of medication, order monitoring to determine the sites and severity of seizures, and work with a neurosurgeon if invasive monitoring is necessary. (Cleveland Clinic pioneered brain-mapping techniques that have made the identification of seizure sites more accurate than ever.)

Specialized *neurosurgeons* collaborate with neurologists to plan and execute procedures and approaches to treat medication-resistant epilepsy.

Psychologists and psychiatrists address the emotional, social, and familial issues surrounding epilepsy and its treatment with medications, talk therapy, biofeedback, and other modalities.

Medical and surgical specialists are supported by *nurses and medical technicians* who are trained in epilepsy treatment and have years of experience in the care of epilepsy patients and their families.

When a patient enters the care path, team members assess each step of his treatment, asking the relevant if-then questions and moving the patient to the next stage of treatment based on the answers. At every stage of the process, caregivers have the option of exercising their own judgment and diverging from the care path based on their knowledge, experience, or "gut feeling." Care paths have highly flexible boundaries and are a continual work in progress.

Once the decision to create a care path for epilepsy was made, it was a simple matter to gather all the people involved in epilepsy care in the same room: neurologists, neurosurgeons, nurses, technicians, administrators, assistants, and medical receptionists. These professionals created a map of what a patient care episode might look like. They charted every place where an individual patient's care might need to diverge from the mainstream and indicated alternative pathways, determined how or why those divergences might have to be taken, and indicated how to respond to them. They also determined the personnel required for every potential occurrence, along with the equipment and supplies that would be needed and their cost. They identified not only multiple points of entry to the care path, but also points of exit, directing patients who were found to have a nonepileptic disorder out of the Epilepsy Center and toward those caregivers who would be more appropriate for their condition. They incorporated patient experience into their calculations, designing the care path to minimize wait times, travel between offices and treatment rooms, and other sources of patient discomfort or frustration.

Before implementation of the care path in the Epilepsy Center, the average time between diagnosis and surgery was 7 months. Of that time, 11.5 days was devoted to direct patient care. A deeper analysis identified every point in the process at which the patient's wait time could be reduced and treatment made more focused; this ultimately reduced the time for direct patient care to 9 days and the time between entry to the Epilepsy Center and the day of surgery to an average of 3.5 months—half as long as it used to take.

Creating a care path would be exceedingly difficult with the kinds of silos and fiefdoms typically found in big organizations. "The administrative structure supported by the institute helps immensely in creating the collaboration we need when designing a care path," said Dr. Imad Najm, director of the Epilepsy Center. Dr. Michael Modic, chairman of the Neurological Institute, shared this view: "A care path is a complex, multidisciplinary instrument that provides guidelines on how people are taken care of over time. Your entire culture has to build it, and when you put it in place, it *changes* your culture for the better. Because the institute is fundamentally multidisciplinary, it enables the input and involvement of a large and complex team. I'm not saying that there aren't other organizational structures that could work and allow you to collaborate like we have, but I do think our institute's format allows us to do things with care paths and many other dimensions of care that don't happen elsewhere. To me, it's intuitively obvious that entities like our institutes are the wave of the future in medicine."

TEAMS TAME SEIZURES

Kelly Labby was working on her computer when her hand began to tremble. "Oh, no," she thought. "I don't think I can stop it." Then everything went blank. She awoke on the floor with her head trapped between her desk and the wall. "It was horrible," she recalls. "My head hurt so badly. And I was all alone." Kelly had had what tens of thousands of North Americans experience every year: a grand mal epileptic seizure.

Epilepsy is not a mental disorder; it's an electrical problem. Most seizures happen when a localized part of the brain's electric circuits goes temporarily haywire. Seizures can range in intensity from a mild change in awareness or sensation to knockdown convulsions such as the one that felled Kelly. In many cases, the cause of epilepsy is unknown. However, Kelly's seizures could be traced to a rare brain tumor that she had developed in early adulthood. She'd been taking medication to control the seizures, but it was clearly not working.

After her grand mal seizure, Kelly moved in with her parents, gave up driving, and worked from home as much as possible. "It was really difficult giving up my independence," she says. "But the thought of being alone again during a grand mal seizure scared me."

For seizures that do not respond to medication, surgery has proved to be an excellent alternative. Most commonly, surgeons remove the part of the brain where the seizures are occurring. But there's a catch: since there are so many critical functions crowded so closely together in the brain, a millimeter's misjudgment can have catastrophic consequences.

Previously, Kelly had resisted having surgery. After the grand mal seizure, though, she asked her doctor for a referral. Her doctor sent her to the Epilepsy Center in Cleveland Clinic's Neurological Institute, where she came under the care of a multispecialty team.

Upon arriving at Cleveland Clinic, Kelly's first stop was the Epilepsy Monitoring Unit. There, electrodes were placed on her scalp. An elaborate computer array recorded her seizures and made it possible to locate the general area of her brain where they were occurring. The news wasn't good. The seizures were coming from just behind the hippocampus, the brain's speech and memory center. A wrong move here could reduce her memory function by up to 30 percent. As a successful government attorney, Kelly did not want to risk an outcome that would endanger her career.

The next step, then, was to locate the seizure site even more precisely so that absolutely no unnecessary tissue would be removed. The first time her seizures were monitored, electrodes were placed in an array on the outside of the head— across the scalp, forehead, and temples. For this more precise and granular monitoring, neurosurgeons placed an electrode grid (developed at Cleveland Clinic) *inside* her skull—under the bone, right next to the brain.

The information supplied by these implanted electrodes allowed surgeons to pinpoint her seizure site with microscopic precision. Dr. William Bingaman of Cleveland Clinic's Neurological Institute performed a successful surgery, removing only the affected tissue and leaving the greater part of the memory and speech centers intact.

After a year of recovery and cognitive and speech therapy, Kelly says that she is thrilled to have her life back. "My thinking is clearer, and my verbal skills are actually stronger than before," she reports. "But while before the surgery I used to work until 11:30 at night, now I spend my evenings helping people who are disabled. The people who cared for me were so generous. I want to give that back somehow."

The Wondrous New Face of Medicine

In 2004, a shotgun blast destroyed most of Connie Culp's face: her right eye, her cheeks, her nose, and part of her mouth. She lost the ability to smell, open her mouth, or even breathe normally.

In a series of 30 surgeries, doctors reconstructed Connie's face, yet she still couldn't breathe, eat, or smell. In 2008, Connie received the first near-total face transplant in the United States at Cleveland Clinic. The procedure began at 5:30 p.m., when doctors checked Connie's blood vessels within the neck region to ensure that she was capable of receiving the transplant. At 8 p.m., surgeons began recovering the facial tissue from the donor, Anna Kasper, who had suffered a massive heart attack and had been declared brain-dead. The more-than-nine-hour surgery paid special attention to maintaining arteries, veins, and nerves, along with soft tissue and bony structures, to preserve circulation and the integrity of the facial graft.

In an adjacent operating room, a second surgical team prepared Connie, removing scar tissue to create a space for the facial graft inset. The donor's facial tissue was transferred to Connie's operating room at 5:10 the next morning. Over the next two hours and 40 minutes, surgeons connected Connie's blood vessels to the facial graft vessels in order to restore blood circulation in her reconstructed face. This was the most critical part of the surgery, because when blood flow from the recipient reaches the graft, immediate rejection may occur. In this case, though, the tissue turned pink, signifying a successful transplantation.

At this point, surgeons still had nearly nine hours of surgery ahead of them to complete the graft attachments, including microsurgical connections of arteries, veins, and nerves. During the entire transplantation procedure, surgeons took turns at the operating table so that they could rest, sleep, or share their expertise. By 4:30 p.m., Connie was wheeled out of the operating room in stable condition. Surgeons had replaced 80 percent of her face in what was the largest and most complex face transplant in the world up until that time. The procedure integrated different functional components such as the nose and lower eyelids, as well as different tissue types, including skin, muscles, bony structures, arteries, veins, and nerves.

The transplant team was led by Dr. Maria Siemionow, Cleveland Clinic's director of plastic surgery research and head of microsurgery training. A highly regarded scientist, Dr. Siemionow has dedicated her professional life to researching and developing methods that doctors could use to substantially help patients with severe facial disfiguration. "As a physician, one of the most rewarding things we can do is to restore a patient's quality of life," said Dr. Siemionow. "Patients with facial disfigurement have very difficult challenges in society. We hope that one day we may be able to help the tens of thousands of patients who are quietly suffering."

The operation that Connie Culp received was an example of extraordinary teamwork across disciplines. Cleveland Clinic's Dermatology & Plastic Surgery Institute led the face transplant surgery, partnering with the Head & Neck Institute. Staff members from psychology and psychiatry, bioethics, social work, anesthesia, transplant, nursing, infectious disease, dentistry, ophthalmology, pharmacy, environmental services, and security also contributed expertise.

But the teamwork had actually begun years before Connie was injured. Dr. Siemionow began experimenting with face transplants on rats, working with a team of researchers to develop many models of transplantation and test many strategies for preventing the body's immune system from rejecting the transplanted bone, skin, and blood vessels. Before approval to perform an experimental face transplant on a human being could be obtained, surgeons had to plan the surgery, the transplant team had to coordinate postoperative care, psychologists had to evaluate prospective patients for suitability, and social workers had to weigh in on what family support a patient would need afterward.

· On Saturdays and Sundays over several months, Dr. Siemi-onow organized more than 40 mock cadaver studies with col-leagues in multiple disciplines, during which they ran through the procedures. She and her colleagues used this time to differentiate tasks, such as who would work on the donor, who would work on the recipient, and how long each step could be expected to take. The final decision to proceed with Connie's transplant was made in a room with leaders from all parts of the team present. All of them had to agree and provide input about Connie's suitability as a re-cipient.

Dr. Frank A. Papay, chairman of the Dermatology & Plastic Surgery Institute, explained, "This work started with a medical team that had an extraordinary vision for what could be possible for patients who have suffered severe trauma to their faces. Cleve-land Clinic's team has worked together to take that vision and make it a reality."

The medical profession is becoming increasingly team-oriented, led by large, physician-run group practices. Patients can help hasten change by paying close attention to how well their doctors are coordinating with other doctors, and they can choose cross-disciplinary institutes for treatment whenever possible. But perhaps the most important thing patients can do at this point is simply to have renewed faith in American medicine, knowing that deep inside some of the largest medical centers, change is happen-ing. More and more doctors today are putting aside their petty interests and squabbles and focusing on what patients need. They're working together in innovative ways to deliver the best care, pio-neer new treatments, and constantly improve their practice of med-icine. And in some cases, teamwork is working miracles, resulting in treatments that would have been unthinkable a few years ago. No one knows that better than Connie Culp.

Care Should Be Monitored and Recorded for Quality

few blocks from Cleveland Clinic's main campus, a vast white-walled space that formerly housed the Cleveland Museum of Contemporary Art is home to a company called Explorys. The employees are young and driven. They gather around one another's laptops and zip between meetings on Razor scooters. In a space that once showcased the most avant-garde painters and sculptors, these information engineers are forging a new kind of cutting edge—a revolution in the use of knowledge that will shape the future of healthcare.

The seed for Explorys was planted when a young physician and self-described "health IT nut" named Dr. Anil Jain came to Cleveland Clinic from Chicago for training in internal medicine. He arrived at a pivotal time in the 1990s, as Cleveland Clinic was in the initial stages of completely digitizing our patient records system—in retrospect, an enormous commitment. At the time, some small groups and hospitals were making forays into digital records, but no academic medical center of any size or stature was willing or prepared to "go all the way."

Appreciating the significance of this commitment requires an understanding of the massive amount of space needed to house the organization's paper medical records. It was an enormous basement area the size of a football field, filled with endless aisles of shelves jammed with folders containing the paper medical records of every patient who had visited Cleveland Clinic since 1921.

When Dr. Jain arrived at Cleveland Clinic, medical records personnel were still responding to requests for patient files by piling the folders into wheeled bins that traveled from floor to floor on metal tracks like cars in a mine shaft. Digitizing all the files would eliminate this cumbersome method of transport and the need to expand the shelving to accommodate an endless number of folders. The electronic medical record system would include putting a computer in every examination room, so that doctors could retrieve and add to patient records with a few keystrokes. All the information in the gigantic warehouse could be stored on a server the size of a household freezer.

Dr. Jain understood that the data stored in the electronic medical records not only were useful for immediate patient care but would also provide medical researchers with a wealth of knowledge. How would male patients between the ages of 50 and 60 with high blood pressure and a family history of diabetes respond to a particular drug regimen, administered in a particular way under certain specified conditions? How long would a patient who has had a given procedure need to stay in the hospital to heal? Before the advent of electronic medical records, there was really no way to answer such questions. The data had been buried; now they could be brought to light. To help access those data, Dr. Jain developed a Google-like search engine called eResearch that enabled Cleveland Clinic doctors and scientists to scour hundreds of thousands of patient records in seconds to find specific pieces of information that they needed for their work.

The electronic patient records used for research are stripped of all names and identifying characteristics, reduced to pure numbers, and combined with similarly stripped records into larger and larger bundles until they become that useful mass of anonymous bits known as "big data." To clarify, electronic patient records are not public property; they are private between the patient and his doctor, hospital, or other medical provider. Stringent rules dictate that only members of a patient's immediate care team can view these records; unauthorized use results in instant dismissal. Cleveland Clinic takes patient privacy seriously, and so does the federal government, whose Health Insurance Portability and Accountability Act (HIPAA) rules reinforce providers' already strong incentives to keep patient records secure.

Around the time Dr. Jain was developing eResearch, he met digital entrepreneur Stephen McHale, who had already founded and sold two companies that focused on the use of massively scaled data for the telecom and other industries. He and his partner, Charlie Lougheed, were looking for fresh entrepreneurial pursuits. They formed a quick friendship with Dr. Jain and started Explorys. "We always talked about applying big data to healthcare," Charlie said, "and the timing was just right. By the time we formed the company, medicine had already entered a perfect storm of unsustainable cost increases, mass proliferation of electronic medical records, and rising expectations for higher quality and cost efficiency among consumers and payers. . . . It was clear to us that this represented a huge opportunity to help do some real good in the world."[1]

Cleveland Clinic provided Explorys with office space and seed money. Stephen and Charlie licensed Dr. Jain's application and scaled it up, using a new architecture that could handle even more data from more sources. Eventually, Explorys grew into an enormous version of the search engine that Dr. Jain had developed for eResearch. Whereas Dr. Jain's original program searched only Cleveland Clinic's electronic medical records, Explorys searches what the company literature describes as "14 major integrated healthcare systems with over 100 billion data elements, 40 million cared-for lives, 200 hospitals and over 100,000 providers."[2]

The hospital systems and providers that initially subscribed to Explorys were connected to a highly secure device behind their computer firewall from which they could access the records of patients at their own institution. What happened next was unthinkable to anyone who is familiar with the hodgepodge of electronic medical records systems used by different hospitals (there are dozens). Explorys mapped all the major electronic medical records systems and understood the unique vocabulary of each. It translated these various languages into a single vocabulary that could be accessed from a single source, activating billions of bits of information that might have been lying dormant in hospital silos and putting them to use for better patient care. Explorys also enables healthcare providers to mine data on costs, supplies, payers, and other operational factors.

Explorys represents a trend that will have an increasing impact on healthcare over the next few decades: the gradual global convergence of digital health information. For the first time, it's technically possible to plug every doctor, every patient, and every hospital, university, and laboratory in the world into a single healthcare data system. The power of such a unified system to improve health and fight disease is almost beyond imagining. It would equal or surpass any breakthrough in medical history.

What could a digital resource on this scale do for doctors and researchers? They would be able to tell at a glance which treatments work and which don't for any specific disease. It would eliminate accidental deaths from drug interactions, overdoses, or lost records. Links between genetic characteristics and specific diseases would be easy to spot. Research could be performed on virtual populations numbering in the millions, going back as many years as there are existing records. A doctor's office would be connected to the whole world, and any patient's health history and medical records could be confidentially accessed at any time from any location.

At the most fundamental level, data and information technology promise to transform medicine from what it has long been—an art—into much more of a rigorous, objective science. Of course, medicine will always continue to be an art, at least in part; each doctor has a unique set of perceptions, personality, skill, experience, and humanity, and many physical processes don't lend themselves to easy measurement or present obvious points of numeric reference.

Data points can be developed for almost anything. Any process can be benchmarked and have goals set and improvement measured. Doctors can figure out what works best in most cases and put that into practice. They can know considerably more about individual patients, diseases, and medical interventions than even the most experienced doctors of days past. This is data-driven medicine, and it's taking the lead in the race for better patient care.

Electronic Medical Records Offer Significant Advantages

Data have long been revered at Cleveland Clinic, which has built one of the nation's most comprehensive electronic medical record (EMR) systems and, as of 2013, had invested about $1 billion in information technology—$400 million in the EMR system alone. The EMR system links Cleveland Clinic doctors, community healthcare affiliates, nurses, and other caregivers at 75 sites across northeastern Ohio, Florida, Nevada, Canada, and Abu Dhabi. Any authorized Cleveland Clinic caregiver can instantly access any patient's record at any of these locations. Caregivers are automatically alerted to dangerous drug interactions and other safety issues, handwritten orders have been replaced by legible text, and the transition from caregiver to caregiver is seamless.

As of 2012, the EMR system contained more than 6 million patient records, and physicians had used the system to give orders more than 240 million times.[3] About 1.5 million patients were able to access portions of their own medical record at home through an ultrasecure web portal. Patients can make appointments, fill prescriptions, and communicate with their doctors' offices online. Their doctors can share lab results and prompt patients to schedule preventive screenings and checkups, while community physicians who refer patients to Cleveland Clinic can track their patients' care online in real time. The system even automatically notifies a doctor if a patient qualifies for one of Cleveland Clinic's ongoing clinical trials. And patients with a chronic disease can be monitored in real time from their own homes.

Both doctors and patients have found the EMR critically important and a huge improvement over paper records. One patient, Amy, had had two brain tumors as a child and grew up being monitored by a multidisciplinary coordinated care team. She visited her providers often and took many medications to maintain her ongoing wellness. She was able to use Cleveland Clinic's online patient record portal to schedule appointments with her many physicians, request prescription refills, and keep track of her own test results and health trends. But the EMR was not just convenient, as Amy discovered when she needed to be seen in the Emergency Department. The care team asked for a list of all the medications she was taking. "The list is long," Amy recalled, "and I couldn't remember every prescription or the specific doses, especially at such a stressful time. I was able to log on to the EMR using my smartphone and access the information when I needed it most."

The EMR has proved invaluable to physicians as well. Dr. William Morris, a Cleveland Clinic hospitalist and self-described "technology geek," provided one example of how the EMR has helped him.

One morning, Dr. Morris was leading rounds with two other doctors when he was notified that his team should prepare to receive a patient who was being transferred from another hospital. The patient had chronic obstructive pulmonary disease (COPD), a respiratory condition that is usually caused by smoking. COPD devastates the air passages and air sacs of the lungs, restricting the amount of oxygen that a patient can process. It is a leading cause of death, with no cure short of lung transplant.

Dr. Morris had planned to see the patient once she had been settled in, but that changed when one of the intake nurses contacted a member of Dr. Miller's team with a terse comment on the patient's condition: "She doesn't look good." Dr. Morris halted rounds and hurried downstairs. "When you hear something like that from a seasoned nurse, you drop everything," he said.

Nurses and respiratory therapists were already hard at work. The patient was a 70-year-old woman with a severe respiratory infection. She was pale and clearly oxygen-starved, her lips pursed as she struggled to take even the shallowest breath. Dr. Morris noted that her blood pressure was stable, but her heart was racing, her oxygen levels were dropping perilously, and oxygen deprivation was affecting her cognitive and speaking abilities.

There were well-established processes for treating a patient in this condition: the team could either administer oxygen on the spot or admit the patient to an ICU to have a breathing tube put in. Before deciding on the proper course of action, Dr. Morris needed more information. Only a half hour earlier, the patient had been discharged by one of Cleveland Clinic's community hospitals. What had her oxygen requirements been there? Did she have heart failure? Critical data that could guide her treatment and avoid medical error were missing. At most hospitals, this information would be part of the patient's paper medical record, possibly buried among reams of other data.

There was no time to consult paper charts. Dr. Morris had to decide right away how to treat the patient. "I suspected that high carbon dioxide was the problem," he said. "That was contributing to her confusion. The higher the carbon dioxide levels, the worse your breathing and the more confused you get. It quickly becomes a vicious cycle, and you have to break it fast."

Fortunately, in addition to being a hospitalist, Dr. Morris was associate chief medical information officer at Cleveland Clinic, a position that gave him a bird's-eye view of the EMR rollout across the system. He knew that the community hospital that had discharged the patient had recently gone live with the EMR, so before reaching for the oxygen mask, he reached for a computer mouse. And there it was on the screen—all the information he needed.

Scanning the patient's medications, doctors' orders, notes, and test results, he saw what respiratory therapy she'd already had, her cardiological workup, and a note about her lungs. He was able to review her full medical history and learn the strategy that her previous doctors had used to treat her. "It's important to know where patients are right now," he said, "but it's also important to know where they were yesterday."

The patient's issues were clear. Her oxygen deficit was being caused by too much carbon dioxide in the blood. If the carbon dioxide continued to crowd out the oxygen, there was a risk of cardiac arrest and death. This patient needed pure oxygen right away. The team placed a positive pressure mask over her mouth and nose, which forced oxygen into her lungs. It didn't take long for her condition to improve. The color returned to her cheeks, and her confusion vanished.

"What happened there was amazing on so many levels," said Dr. Morris. "Thanks to the EMR, we were able to spare her the painful and invasive ordeal of a breathing tube. We didn't have to work her up to learn a lot of things that her previous doctors had already found out. We didn't have to duplicate services and waste time and resources. The real power of the EMR is that it gives us a comprehensive picture of our patient—instantly. In this case, it told me so much about the patient that the residents working that day thought I'd seen and treated her previously." As EMR technology develops, systems will become far more powerful and easier to use. They will increasingly provide decision support, giving physicians and other healthcare providers guidance on whether to order particular tests or interventions. One such system at Massachusetts General Hospital has helped doctors decide when to perform imaging studies on patients. Research has found that doctors using the system ordered fewer unnecessary tests.[4]

Geisinger Health System incorporated into its EMR system a set of best practices relating to the care of patients receiving elective cardiac bypass surgery. Doctors received reminders and tools to help them implement the best practices, which were based on both evidence and the doctors' expert opinions. Geisinger saw a 67 percent drop in mortality and a 1.3-day decrease in the length of hospital stays. Costs for each patient dropped by almost 5 percent.[5]

EMRs will soon be able to make predictions, based on scientific evidence, concerning the outcomes of particular interventions. Before a doctor orders a medication for a patient, she will know that there is, for instance, a 75 percent likelihood that it will yield the desired result, as compared with a 65 percent likelihood for a second medication and a 42 percent likelihood for a third. EMRs will also soon help clinicians do things that seem straight out of science fiction.

Artificial Limbs That "Talk"

One of the trends in technology is known as "the Internet of Things," which refers to the embedding of computers and mobile communication technology into physical objects in daily life. Smartphones are already pervasive, and Google has smart glasses. Soon almost everything, from cars to clothing to furniture, will be "smart." The potential applications of this technology to medicine are exciting. What if patients had smart artificial legs or hips? The sensors implanted in the artificial limb or joint would create a constant stream of data about such things as activity, range of motion, and ability to carry weight. That information would be sent to the patient's doctors and filed in his EMR. Doctors would be able to monitor each patient's progress in real time, noticing trends and preventing problems before patients became aware of them. They could also create customized physical therapy programs for patients based on their unique utilization profile (how they actually use the artificial limb or joint). With smart implants, EMRs are poised to usher in a whole new level of patient-doctor communication, revolutionizing the care provided across the healthcare spectrum.

Mainstreaming the EMR

Ideally, such tantalizing possibilities will inspire more doctors and America's healthcare system as a whole to embrace EMRs. In countries such as the Netherlands, New Zealand, and Norway, doctors have for years almost entirely dispensed with paper and gone digital.[6] As of 2013, most American hospitals don't use EMRs. Some have digitized parts of their caregiving, but fewer than 2 percent of hospitals have what the government calls a "complete electronic medical record."[7] Dr. C. Martin Harris, chief information officer of Cleveland Clinic, estimated that fewer than 20 percent of all physicians' offices use EMRs to write orders, document care, write prescriptions, capture diagnostic images, and perform computer-assisted support (for example, identify all patients who need a certain blood test).

Cost has been a big problem. Patients and insurance companies benefit from the higher-quality and more efficient care that EMRs afford, but for doctors in private practice, EMRs have seemed like another big capital investment, the cost of which is difficult to recoup.

Doctors have also wondered about the usefulness of EMRs given the fragmentation of America's healthcare system and the fact that competing EMR systems haven't been able to talk to each other. A local dermatologist might invest in one EMR system, only to find that a group of internists in her area uses a different system, a group of surgeons uses a third system, and the nearby community hospital has no EMR system. In this context, making a large investment in the technology hasn't always seemed to make sense.[8] Some doctors have called for the government or some other authority to establish a standard EMR format to ensure that everybody is on the same page.[9] Opponents of such a move worry that the government might not be competent to make the best choice or that the establishment of a standard format would halt the development of new and possibly better formats.

The good news is that doctors and hospitals are finally starting to overcome their misgivings and adopt EMR technology. Buried in the 2009 federal economic stimulus package was a provision authorizing the government to dispense additional Medicare and Medicaid money to doctors and hospitals that used EMRs in a significant way, known in the industry as "meaningful use." The government designated seven stages of meaningful use corresponding to different things that doctors could do using EMRs, such as prescribing medications or checking for insurance eligibility.[10] Between 2009 and 2011, the percentage of hospitals with some form of EMR roughly doubled, rising from 16 to 35 percent. As of 2012, the government had paid out more than $3 billion to 2,000 hospitals and more than 41,000 private doctors who met the criteria.[11] The number of hospitals and independent medical practices using some form of EMR is expected to rise dramatically in the coming years as the government requires higher levels of meaningful use to qualify for the incentive money.

The story of the EMR reveals some of the important advantages of large, physician-run group practices. Organizations such as Cleveland Clinic were at the forefront in adopting information technology for a couple of reasons. First, they had the financial resources required to make the up-front investments that EMR technology required. Systems cost as much as $25,000 per doctor—a price that many independent doctors in private practice couldn't afford. Kaiser Permanente spent $4 billion getting its system online, linking almost 16,000 doctors and 9 million patients.[12]

Second, because all the doctors were part of one organization, operating within a single corporate structure, that organization was able to determine which EMR system to buy for the entire establishment and then coordinate the complex task of rolling it out across hundreds of offices. Some non-group practice hospitals have six to eight different EMR systems covering different medical specialties or operational areas.[13] At one more traditional Ohio hospital system, groups of physicians within the entity purchased different, incompatible systems. An internist at the hospital reported carrying around 10 passwords that were required to log in to the different systems. Incompatibility issues were so profound that some doctors refused to use EMR technology to order prescriptions.[14] As a large, physician-run group practice, Cleveland Clinic didn't have these kinds of problems. Size and corporate structure have become even more important as medicine has entered the digital age. Even with government support, it's not clear that smaller, independent practices will implement EMR systems.

Ultimately, a single, unified EMR system will probably link hospitals and other clinics around the country. Already companies are increasingly making specific EMR systems that are able to converse with one another, and over the next few years, more doctors and hospitals undoubtedly will come together to integrate their systems. In the slightly longer term, EMRs will improve not merely the quality of care but ultimately its cost, which should encourage further investment. Hospitals will find that they are able to reduce duplicate or wasteful procedures thanks to EMRs. Patients will better engage with their healthcare, enabling the prevention of more of the chronic illnesses that presently account for 70 percent of the nation's expenditures on healthcare. Hospitals will prevent drug interactions from taking place, reducing the cost of caring for patients who have had adverse reactions. And as more healthcare providers move toward data-driven care, where computers help doctors make decisions in real time, patients will enjoy better outcomes, further reducing the cost of treatment.

Big Data Drive Medical Research and Improve Healthcare Outcomes

The reluctance of some healthcare providers to support data-driven medicine has stemmed from a fear that doing so would make the healthcare experience less personal—that doctors would make decisions based on statistics rather than on in-depth assessments of patients as individuals. The experience at Cleveland Clinic suggests that this fear is unfounded. Data are no substitute for one-on-one consideration of a patient's unique symptoms and history. Data-driven medicine is helpful as an *adjunct* to the physician's experience and intuition, but it is not a replacement for it. When it is used in a limited and thoughtful way, data-driven medicine allows care providers to achieve an even *deeper* understanding of the patient's unique history and characteristics. That's because data-driven medicine and the EMR enable providers to compare the individual patient with numerous other patients in the aggregate.

Comparisons using big medical data have been occurring at Cleveland Clinic for decades. Its thoracic surgery and cardiovascular surgery departments were among the first in the country to collect large amounts of data, even before the widespread use of computers and the Internet. Doctors there developed coronary artery bypass surgery in the late 1960s. By 1970, they realized that they were accumulating a unique quantity of data on this technique that could be of value to them and others going forward. They started keeping meticulous records of each patient and each surgery and its outcomes, using punch cards to enter this information and depositing those records in what was then a sophisticated computerized registry called the Cardiovascular Information Registry. Compiling data on demographics, treatments, lab work, and outcomes for thousands of patients required a significant financial outlay. The organization went to great lengths to ensure that the data were as accurate and complete as possible, even using private detectives to track down former patients and find out how they were faring many years after their surgeries.

Cleveland Clinic went to such great lengths to assemble this information because we were one of the few hospitals that could. Coronary bypass was the first procedure we offered to help patients with clogged arteries. At the time of this technique's inception, doctors didn't know whether people who had coronary bypass did better over time than people who didn't in terms of their life expectancy, complications, and quality of life. They also didn't know which kinds of patients benefited from surgical intervention. Treating individual patients with coronary bypass involved a great deal of guesswork for doctors, and the same remains true today in other areas of medicine.

Because Cleveland Clinic was the only hospital performing a significant number of coronary bypasses at that time, we were the only one that could collect a large volume of data. The registry enabled doctors to confirm that some patients who had coronary bypasses did much better than those who didn't have the surgery or who underwent other kinds of heart surgery. They learned which kind of bypass operation worked best and came to understand what would happen to patients over time if the blockages in their arteries went untreated. All these findings changed surgical procedures. A seminal paper reporting the data was published in 1973,[15] and coronary artery bypass surgery became the most performed heart operation in the world.

Cleveland Clinic began to expand the registry as we treated more and more patients. We modernized data collection and continued to follow up with patients up to 25 years after their surgeries, providing a much better picture of how the surgery might have led to complications such as bleeding or strokes. Consequently, doctors were able to refine bypass surgery based on an ever-improving understanding of what worked and what didn't.

They also could use the registry to study and improve other lifesaving heart surgeries. Mitral valve replacement is one of the great success stories of cardiac surgery. The mitral valve controls blood flow inside the left ventricle of the heart. It has two leaflets that open and close, and these leaflets are subject to several disorders. They can become loose and floppy or stiff and fibrous, causing blood to leak in and out when it isn't supposed to. The heart has to work harder to overcome the effects of the leak, and over time this can result in heart failure.

Fortunately, mitral valves can be replaced. Until the mid- to late 1990s, people in their sixties or seventies who were already very sick were having mitral valve replacements. Yet the valves lasted only about 10 years before they broke down. Then doctors at Cleveland Clinic discovered that they could repair patients' diseased valves instead of replacing them. Repairing a valve would be much less invasive than replacing it, and patients would have considerably fewer complications down the road. And repairs done at a younger age, before patients became really sick with heart disease, would greatly reduce the risks of surgery.

Thanks to Cleveland Clinic's registry, doctors could compare patients who had received repairs with those who got replacements. The hard data demonstrated that patients who had had repairs experienced results that were as good as, if not better than, those experienced by people whose valves had been replaced. Those results were published in a series of medical papers during the 1990s, changing the treatment of this condition for thousands of patients.

As of 2013, the registry includes data on more than 220,000 patients. Cleveland Clinic spends about $1 million a year maintaining it, and several dozen people work on it full time. The clinic uses the registry to report on the quality of our care to the state of Ohio and to answer questions from patients and insurers, but mainly it's used to push clinical research forward. Based at least in part on data from the registry, in 2012 a small group of investigators in cardiothoracic surgery published 111 journal articles, 30 book chapters, and 3 books. The quality of the data is so good that the department receives about 300 requests per year from other Cleveland Clinic researchers who want to use it.

The resulting studies have made major contributions to clinical care, and not just for heart patients. One group of doctors used the registry to create a staging framework for esophageal cancer. They needed to understand precisely how the disease unfolded to determine the best course of treatment for particular patients. "Until now, for esophageal cancer, all the estimates we had about the risk of patients at different points in time were just guesswork," said Dr. Eugene Blackstone, a chief collaborator in this research. "We suspected that what doctors were saying was incompatible with the biology of the disease and human anatomy. Our global study, which included data from the registry, let us completely revamp how esophageal cancer is staged." In the near future, doctors will be able to give patients a much better idea of their prognosis at different stages, and also whether radiation, surgery, chemotherapy, or some other treatment is the best option for their particular disease. And they'll be able to do it based not on intuition but on cold, hard data.

As the EMR system expanded, Cleveland Clinic began supplementing data from the registry with large amounts of new patient data. We also launched an initiative called the Knowledge Program that asks patients to electronically enter data about how they are feeling to round out the information in their EMR. Patients who come in for an outpatient visit are handed a tablet and asked to answer a few questions about their illness and their quality of life. As their care proceeds, they're queried again at several points. All these data help our doctors understand patients' ongoing conditions. They can compare what patients report to what they themselves observe and know through the tests they've run. And they can use these results to adjust or modify treatments if necessary. They can also study the results for populations of patients to find useful patterns and trends, including which treatments are most effective and how they might best be administered.

This is just the beginning. A small army of statisticians, computer programmers, and others in Cleveland Clinic's Lerner Research Institute works with clinicians to analyze data and write research articles. Researchers in the Cleveland Clinic network can also access all the data in Explorys and use other tools as well to study and analyze the big data in order to gain new knowledge about patients.

As more institutions make use of big data, the pace of medical research will increase dramatically. Questions about the efficacy of treatments will take weeks or months to answer, not years. Doctors will have answers at their fingertips in real time, applying them as they make treatment decisions. In effect, the line between doctors and researchers will blur as never before. Computers will never replace a physician's own wisdom, but they will enhance that wisdom and allow the doctor to provide proactive care. For instance, rather than wait for patients to come in, physicians can use computers to remind patients that it's time for a checkup or to take certain tests. That's because data from millions of other people with the same condition will have shown that these are helpful actions to take at that point in time.

Explorys CEO Stephen McHale said, "Thanks to big data, there's so much we can do now to improve care. We will see dramatic improvements in outcomes. Chronic conditions such as heart disease and diabetes will be far better managed, giving people a better quality of life. This is evidence-based medicine, thanks to information technology."

Dr. David Levin, chief medical information officer at Cleveland Clinic, predicts that computers and big data will soon allow doctors to function more like air traffic control officials. With scarce resources, doctors can't afford to provide constant care to each of their hundreds or thousands of patients. Thanks to real-time, data-driven insights, however, they will be able to know which of their patients require which interventions or monitoring at specific points in time. "The technology will allow doctors, nurses, and others to home in on patients whose condition is changing rapidly. And thanks to mobile technology, time and space won't matter so much. Doctors will be able to monitor patients in different cities and give them the care they need, when they need it, based on insights from a large group of other patients."

In the near future, patients will be able to go online and find much more usable and accurate information about the likely outcome of whatever treatments they're considering. A patient who is diagnosed with a serious illness today might research it by going online and looking at a hodgepodge of different sites. He might find a journal article or two detailing the latest research, but he won't find a website where he can plug in his test results and get back highly accurate information that says, "Here are your treatment options, and here's what the data say about how likely each of them is to work for someone with your exact profile (age, sex, family history, and so on)."

That's going to change. Soon, a patient will be able to enter her information into a "comprehensive risk calculator" that uses algorithms to calculate the patient's risk of complications or success based on the experience of thousands or even millions of other patients, taking into account all the specifics of the patient's situation. Cleveland Clinic already has some risk calculators online.[16] Although they're intended primarily for doctors, consumers can use them as well. They are part of the exciting future of healthcare, enabled by EMRs and big data.

Fewer Infections and Safer Surgeries

In addition to guiding clinical decisions, big data will improve healthcare through facilitation of the kind of process improvements discussed in previous chapters. Continually updating and improving medical processes requires data in order to demonstrate current outcomes and indicate potential problem areas. As of 2013,

Cleveland Clinic's EMR is giving doctors a whole new window on how they do things. It's the beginning of an era in which quality and efficiency of care across the board will improve as never before.

Ultimately what has driven improvement is economics. The federal government has begun reimbursing doctors not on the basis of how many procedures they do (that is, fee for service) but on the outcomes and the value of the care provided. The government has started to require hospitals to report data on various aspects of their performance (patient mortality, infections, patient experience, and so on). In 2013, 2 to 3 percent of Cleveland Clinic's reimbursement from Medicare is tied to these numbers. In coming years, the measurements used will expand, and about 10 to 20 percent of reimbursements will be tied to performance. New incentives will emerge to encourage the reporting of performance data on individual physicians, as will new penalties for not reporting. These current and expected trends are leading hospitals to use data to help them deliver more value than ever before.

The EMR will help by making possible the collection of much more data about patients and their care. Dr. Shannon Phillips, quality and safety officer at Cleveland Clinic's main campus, said that in hospitals without EMRs or other electronic systems, data tend to fall through the cracks. By contrast, EMRs automatically track test results and other pieces of data related to patient care. According to Dr. Phillips, "If you can't depend on automated systems, then you are really at the mercy of caregivers who input data manually. Today's hospitals are doing a good job of tracking certain measures that the government requires us to report on in order to maintain payments. That's where their focus is. But other measures that may not be required, but are nevertheless important, may not receive as much attention. Hospitals also may not spend as much time as they could stepping back, analyzing the data, and actively figuring out how to make care better. That's where our emphasis has to be going forward."

Like many other hospitals, Cleveland Clinic has been paying close attention to reporting on the government-mandated measures, and it's made a difference. Patients in Cleveland Clinic's hospitals are much safer in 2013 than they were just 10 years earlier. A good example is central line infections, which are associated with the insertion of an IV tube and needle into a large blood vessel of the neck, chest, or groin. These infections are quite serious, and it used to be that as many as a quarter of the patients who got them died.

But the number of central line infections has fallen. In 2009, Cleveland Clinic saw 8 central line infections in its intensive care units for every 1,000 patient line days (a line day is a day in which a single patient had a line inserted). Just three years later, that number had fallen to less than 2 central line infections per 1,000 line days.

All told, Cleveland Clinic avoided 27,000 patient deaths and saved $1.8 billion in costs associated with treating these infections. It did so by collecting data on line infections, identifying the procedures that were contributing to the problem, and creating new protocols (such as increasing the use of latex gloves and changing the way catheters are inserted).[17] Guido Bergomi, senior director of quality improvement at Cleveland Clinic, recalled that the first step was to form a multidisciplinary team that represented physicians in the intensive care units. "We got traction because we really cared about improving, and the data we had were very visible. The people who were doing the actual work helped figure out how to change our processes. A role played by the members of my team was making sure that the data we were reporting made sense to them, were useful, and were timely." Nationally, central line infections in intensive care units have dropped by 60 percent since 2001.

Cleveland Clinic has also used EMR technology to improve patient safety during surgery. During the mid-2000s, as a participant in the American College of Surgeons' National Surgical Quality Improvement Program, we learned that although our mortality rate for surgery patients was fairly low compared with the rates at other hospitals, our complication rates were higher than desired. When compared with surgery patients at other hospitals, Cleveland Clinic's patients were having higher rates of surgical site infections, urinary tract infections, and clots in their veins, among other complications.

Collecting data enabled the doctors to drill down and look more closely at what was going on. Which surgical procedures had the highest rates of complications? Which complications occurred most frequently? Which patients were primarily affected? The answers to these questions led to the implementation of various performance improvement projects and, subsequently, a significant lowering of the rates of surgical site infections and urinary tract infections.

Improving Performance at All Levels

Robust data are essential, but making the most of that information requires a strong culture of quality and improvement—a culture that Cleveland Clinic has consciously fostered. It has an entire institute, the Quality & Patient Safety Institute, that compiles and analyzes data to help the organization continually improve. The Quality & Patient Safety Institute encompasses departments devoted to decreasing the number of patient infections, reducing risks to patients, improving processes, collecting and managing data, and improving patient quality. Most of Cleveland Clinic's hospitals have staff members who are responsible for safety and infection control, and every disease-oriented institute has a physician who serves as its quality control officer and interfaces with the Quality & Patient Safety Institute.

This is yet another example of how large, physician-run group practices can make a difference. Taking these physicians away from their primary job of treating patients costs money, but Cleveland Clinic made the change because doing so served its fundamental mission of putting patients first. "My biggest problem is that I can't keep up with all the quality projects initiated by the quality officers in our institutes," said Quality and Safety Officer Dr. Shannon Phillips. "I might put out a centralized quality directive. Then physicians in the institutes look at the data, analyze them, and prioritize change and improvement. And I get involved again in situations where we want to push quality initiatives across institutes. I help spread what we've learned so that as much of Cleveland Clinic as possible can implement it."

The institutes structure greatly boosted Cleveland Clinic's ability to improve safety and quality. A typical hospital might have a few different departments that perform a certain procedure or treat a certain condition. These departments might not collect the same data or report them in the same way. They also might not come together to aggregate the data.

Over the past decade, Cleveland Clinic has extended its data collection to all clinical areas. And as institutes were established, each became responsible for collecting and reporting its data every year. The institutes structure enables the collection of meaningful information about how providers treated specific diseases or conditions. That information helped in pinpointing areas that required improvement and in devising solutions that transformed the way the entire institution handles whole classes of patients.

The reporting part of this process is crucial. What good are data if an organization fearfully withholds that information? Decades ago, Cleveland Clinic's cardiologists started presenting data from the registry to everyone who was involved in caring for heart patients. They did it every year, and physicians started asking them for copies of the presentations. So they created a booklet containing that information and then decided to share data on Cleveland Clinic's mortality and complication rates with colleagues at other institutions around the country. To them, the benefits outweighed the risks, inasmuch as they hoped to spark a national conversation that would generate new ideas for better treatment. Other providers joined in the effort and contributed their own data, allowing Cleveland Clinic to see how well it was doing in relation to others in the field. It was the beginning of a quality and safety revolution.

Currently, all of Cleveland Clinic's patient care services compile and publish books of their outcomes every year and send out 50,000 printed copies to referring physicians and others. They are like nothing else in healthcare (or any other industry). Each book examines the services and procedures that the institute offers and reports on volumes, outcomes, and mortality. Comparative data are included, along with descriptions of innovative procedures, lists of publications by Cleveland Clinic doctors and researchers, and other information that the institutes believe will help referring physicians and others evaluate the organization. Data include how long patients stay in the hospital for specific procedures, how long patients survive after undergoing various treatments, and how long patients have to wait for certain organ transplants. In effect, Cleveland Clinic voluntarily provides a comprehensive portrait of how well it's doing, even when the outcomes are less than flattering to the organization.

Armed with data, the institutes have been able to make huge strides in standardizing (and thus enhancing) the care they provide. The care paths mentioned in previous chapters have all been based on data collection and reporting within the institutes. Because the doctors who treated a specific disease collaborated on collecting and publishing their data and because they had these at their fingertips, they could look for opportunities to improve care. They made changes, and, over time, both performance and outcomes improved.

Sometimes a specific change wound up having quite a significant impact. Overtreatment, for instance, has been a major driver of healthcare costs, with too many patients receiving treatments that don't benefit them. Avoiding overtreatment requires care providers to find better ways of screening patients to ensure that those who are most likely to benefit from a certain procedure are the ones who get that treatment and that those who wouldn't benefit are steered to other forms of treatment.

Cleveland Clinic care providers applied this approach to the treatment of strokes. Patients who had had certain types of strokes caused by blood clots in the brain were treated using catheters to clear out the brain's blood vessels—a method much like angioplasty for clearing blocked blood vessels in the heart. This technique worked only on some patients, and not on those who had suffered severe strokes. Dr. Shazam Hussain, who heads Cleveland Clinic's stroke program as a member of the Cerebrovascular Center, worked with his team to develop a care path for treating strokes caused by blood clots in the brain. By studying the data on past patient outcomes, the team could see that clearing out blood clots was not helping the patients with severe strokes. But the CT scans that doctors were using to screen patients for the procedure weren't giving them enough information on the stroke's severity, so they added another layer of diagnostics to the care path: giving patients an MRI.

Drawing information from the Knowledge Program and other sources, Dr. Hussain and his team analyzed the outcomes. "Imagine how excited we were," Dr. Hussain said, "to find that we had cut in half the number of procedures that we were doing, even as our outcomes improved substantially." The EMR played a key role in this breakthrough. "The care path structured the way we were inputting data, since caregivers were prompted to input data at various times, and other data, such as test results, went into the EMR automatically. As a team, we could then work with the data to see how well we were treating strokes. Before, the way we practiced medicine was intuitive, kind of hit-or-miss. Now, we have reliable data that we review as a team on a monthly basis. And we're doing this for all dimensions of how we care for stroke victims."

Change Is the Only Constant

The bad news about the state of the healthcare system in America is pervasive, but that's not even close to the whole story. Digital technology has revolutionized industry after industry during the past decade. Although American medicine has come relatively late to the game, the gains thus far have been huge. At Cleveland Clinic, the EMR has integrated the organization's far-flung facilities, enabling detailed examination of quality, safety, and patient experience statistics. Nationwide, the big data provided by EMR systems has given researchers an unprecedented bird's-eye view of the nation's health, allowing them to spot and follow disease trends across many dimensions. Hospital processes are beginning to improve, and physicians are increasingly making medical decisions based on actual data, not just gut feelings.

This evolution must continue. Federal agencies can push all providers to measure what they do and to improve by continuing to provide financial incentives to hospitals that deliver higher-value care. Government also needs to encourage more hospitals and physicians to digitize their practices and to help establish a single standard for EMR systems, so that all systems can talk to one another.

Patients must stay informed. At one time, medical decision making was cloaked in secrecy. Patients couldn't examine their medical records; x-rays were filed away from patients' eyes; and hospitals' outcomes, volumes, and mortality rates were not available, if they were collected at all. Today, patients have access to all this and more. Some hospitals and medical centers have been slow to take advantage of this trend, but the best are realizing that the more patients know, the more they can participate in their healthcare and the better the outcomes and experiences that they'll have will be. Patients who are sick and require medical attention should take the time to research not merely their condition but the performance of potential doctors and hospitals. They also should take advantage of the new opportunities afforded by technology in order to understand their own body and the treatments they receive.

The history of healthcare has moved in progressive stages, each of which can be measured in terms of the longer, more productive lives that individuals have realized. The next stage is here. The technology is now available to create a national system of electronic medical records, one that will take healthcare to a new and powerful level of effectiveness. It will make national healthcare reform not only conceivable, but doable.

Chapter 4

Twenty-First-Century Care Should Be Innovative

What will tomorrow's medical game changers be? Most important, who will bring them into being, and where? The answer to this last question is more than a matter of satisfying curiosity. It could affect the course of people's health for generations.

The developers of medical game changers can be smart, focused, and sometimes intent on their work to the exclusion of everything else. Take, for example, Dr. F. Mason Sones. This brilliant cardiologist launched the modern era of coronary revascularization in 1956 by developing coronary angiography—a technology that allows doctors to see the blockages in blood vessels that cause chest pains and sometimes heart attacks. Dr. Sones could be difficult when he didn't get his way, and he was notoriously indifferent to other people's schedules. Yet he was a gregarious man who liked to share his discoveries with his younger colleagues.

Dr. Sones was good friends with a young surgeon, René Favaloro, who had come to Cleveland Clinic from Argentina in the early

1960s to learn what he could about the developing field of cardiac surgery. When Dr. Favaloro arrived, he had little money and no local friends, but a thirst for discovery. He was surprised at how easily he was accepted as a colleague by the surgical leadership, who urged him to take advantage of Cleveland Clinic's resources for learning and discovery.

Drs. Favaloro and Sones spent hours poring over 16-mm films of coronary angiograms. They were plotting a new surgical approach to coronary artery disease—resolving blockages by cutting out the blocked portion of the artery and replacing it with a blood vessel taken from another part of the body. Dr. Favaloro performed the first published coronary artery bypass in 1967, and this procedure went on to become one of the most widely performed operations in the world. A warm, thoughtful man with a strong humanistic streak, Dr. Favaloro could have stayed in the United States and reaped a fortune from his reputation and his surgical expertise. Instead, he returned to Argentina, where at tremendous personal cost he founded his own heart clinic to bring what he'd learned at Cleveland Clinic to the underserved people of his own country.

Another Cleveland Clinic clinician, researcher, and potential game changer developer, Dr. Stanley Hazen, has made an enormous contribution to the understanding of heart disease in the past decade. He has written more than 200 peer-reviewed articles, invited reviews, and book chapters in the fields of atherosclerosis, oxidation and inflammation chemistry, and cardiovascular disease. In 2012, the National Heart, Lung, and Blood Institute bet $4.7 million of American taxpayers' money that Dr. Hazen would be able to discover new ways to diagnose and cure heart disease, which is still the number one killer of Americans.

The wager seems to have been a sound one. In 2013, Dr. Hazen and his colleague Dr. Wilson Tang made national news by discovering a previously unknown cause of heart disease. They found it not by examining the heart but by looking in the gut—in the stomach and small intestine, where billions of specialized bacteria live off the food that humans eat and have evolved to play a vital role in digestion. Dr. Hazen learned that certain bacteria in the gut live on carnitine, a naturally occurring biochemical compound that is found mostly in red meat, but also in egg yolks. As these bacteria feast on carnitine, they excrete an enzyme called TMAO that makes its way into the blood. TMAO seems to decrease the amount of cholesterol naturally eliminated by the body by 30 percent, and also makes it easier for cholesterol to build up inside the coronary artery walls, thereby increasing the potential for heart attack. The connection between these bacteria and TMAO solves the mystery of why red meat in the diet seems to contribute to heart disease even when the meat is lean or shorn of cholesterol-laden fat.

Dr. Hazen found that the bacteria that consume carnitine actually die off in people who stop eating meat or animal products (vegans). If a vegan decided to eat a hot dog or an egg salad sandwich, the food would pass harmlessly through her system. But if she resumed the regular habit of eating meat, the bacteria in question would reassert themselves, bringing with them renewed cardiogenic risk.

These findings suggest that a powerful and cost-free, though underutilized, way of preventing heart disease would be to eliminate meat and eggs from the diet. But few people care to adopt this preventive approach, even if it would keep them off the operating table. So the search for new antibiotics that can selectively eliminate carnitine-eating bacteria in the gut and allow people to eat meat and eggs without producing TMAO will begin. Before that, there may be a diagnostic test for the presence of coronary artery disease based on measuring the amount of TMAO in the blood. But a great deal of work remains to be done.

A Looming Innovation Crisis?

The past century has been one of remarkable medical progress, but today, medical innovation is facing important challenges. It takes an average of *13 years* for a healthcare innovation to be established as a mainstream standard of care. This excessive lag time may be one reason that inventors are submitting fewer patent applications for new drugs and devices, and that fewer successful products are reaching patients. Ironically, this decline in patent submissions is occurring amid an explosion of knowledge from laboratories and scientific investigators. As an FDA report noted, "At a time when basic biomedical knowledge is increasing exponentially, the gap between bench discoveries and bedside application seems to be expanding."[1] Another observer has remarked, "There are lots of great ideas within academic medical centers—the trick is finding an efficient way to get them out."[2]

There is encouraging news, however. As discussed, large, physician-run group practices are hastening innovation by adopting electronic medical records. A few leading academic medical centers are going much further, centering the practice of medicine on innovation. Medical centers that have traditionally focused on generating knowledge are now paying attention to the marketplace—the primary channel for bringing medical advances to patient bedsides. Medical centers are helping doctors patent and commercialize innovations that arise out of their daily practice. They're adopting strategies for identifying clinical needs, removing obstacles to innovation, and forming new businesses around promising breakthroughs. Medical centers are even retooling medical schools to create a generation of doctor-innovators.

The scope of some of the innovations being developed at Cleveland Clinic would have been unimaginable even two decades ago:

- More effective treatments for diabetes

- Handheld scanners that can detect skin cancer

- A potential vaccine for breast cancer

- Nanoparticles that target cancer cells without affecting nearby healthy tissue

- A therapy to potentially cure certain spinal cord injuries

- A device that uses mild electric pulses to alleviate excruciating cluster headaches

This is from only one institution. With this kind of momentum spreading nationwide, it's easy to imagine the tremendous strides in basic research that can be made using the large amounts of data that are already available to researchers almost instantly. New treatments will begin making a difference in patients' lives only 2 or 3 years after those treatments are conceived, instead of the 13 years it now takes. Millions of patients will benefit in ways that can't be predicted today.

Innovation and Its Enemies

An idea in and of itself is not an innovation. The world is full of ideas that go nowhere. *An innovation is an idea that has been put to work.* The difference between an idea and an innovation is the difference between science and technology: Science is ideas; technology is utility. Science establishes truths; technology solves problems. Science experiments; technology investigates. Science is global; technology addresses a specific situation. Having an idea doesn't make someone an innovator any more than having a brush makes him a painter. As innovation consultant James Barnes said, "Innovation is the conversion of knowledge and ideas into a benefit, which may be for commercial use for the public good."[3]

Unfortunately, the enemies of innovation are powerful. One of the most insidious is an excessive reverence for tradition. For centuries, medicine was one of the most tradition-bound professions. Precedent overruled observation. Generation after generation of doctors performed procedures such as bloodletting without determining whether they actually worked. Even today, hospital administrators have been known to defend outmoded practices by saying, "That's the way we do it," or, "That's the way our founders did it."

Another enemy of innovation is, ironically, success. If something isn't broken, why fix it? Armed with this way of thinking, physicians have often overestimated what was known and underestimated what was yet to be discovered. In 1873, Sir John Erichsen, surgeon to Queen Victoria, declared that "although methods of practice may be modified and varied, and even improved to some extent," surgery had reached the limit of what it could do. "The knife," he said, "cannot always have fresh fields for conquest." How wrong he was. Surgical innovation has continued uninterrupted since that time. One example is coronary artery bypass, which was developed based on new knowledge of the disease mechanism along with improvements in imaging, anesthesia, and extracorporeal oxygenation. Similar examples abound in every surgical specialty.

A third enemy of innovation is the conventional approach to medical education. Traditional medical schools demand that students accumulate a massive quantity of facts. Too often, students learn these facts for the purpose of regurgitation, not application. After graduation, doctors undergoing additional training as medical residents are encouraged to imitate established doctors. They are rewarded for becoming junior versions of the reigning technical and intellectual stars.

A final enemy of innovation is the pressure to reduce costs. In the past, both doctors and patients took it for granted that doctors would do everything that was humanly possible to help a patient. Today, however, in the existing economic and healthcare reform climate, doctors must weigh the cost of treatment against the potential benefit. Modern medicine's ability to treat what ails certain patients exceeds what society is now willing to pay—a reality that is at the heart of every major healthcare issue today.

Turbocharging Academic Medical Centers

Overcoming these enemies in order to unleash the medical field's full capacity for innovation has to be addressed at the institutional level by building on the strengths of the academic medical center. Places such as Cleveland Clinic, Mayo Clinic, and Johns Hopkins are notable in that they combine patient care, research, and education. They are priceless assets of the healthcare infrastructure and can be a paradise for inventors.

At academic medical centers, patients produce data that drive research. Research produces concepts that inspire innovation. Finally, and most valuably, innovators collaborate with their end users—not as customers but as colleagues. It's a complete feedback loop from bench to bedside and back again—with a side trip to the classroom for graduate medical education. At the center of it all is the patient, the inspiration for and principal beneficiary of all this work.

At their best, academic medical centers are defined by a strong culture of innovation in which collaboration, risk, openness, and idea sharing are the norm. Ideas are exposed to diverse opinions. New notions live or die based on their ability to achieve practical application.

Cleveland Clinic has a remarkably strong and resilient culture of innovation, in part because that's the culture that was instilled by the founders. Both basic and clinical research have been fundamental to Cleveland Clinic's mission from the beginning. The founders were convinced that they could provide the best patient care only by conducting active programs of medical research in their new clinic. In 1921, they agreed that no less than one-fourth of the net income from the new organization would be devoted to research and indigent care. Later, this percentage was substantially increased, and in 1928, the trustees approved the construction of a building for medical research.

All of Cleveland Clinic's founders engaged in research, but George Crile was its strongest advocate. He believed that laboratory discoveries provided the essential scientific basis for modern clinical practice. His investigations led to his original thesis linking the activity of the adrenal glands to physiologic stress. Throughout the twentieth century, research and innovation flourished. The organization's long list of medical "firsts" provides a glimpse into some of the numerous breakthroughs at Cleveland Clinic over the years. These include, among many others:

- The first surgical removal of the larynx (1920s)

- The first successful human-to-human blood transfusion (1920s)

- The isolation of angiotensin and serotonin, key factors in hypertension (1940s)

- The first identification of carpal tunnel syndrome and the development of a diagnostic test for the condition (1951)

- A pioneering "stopped heart" open heart surgery (1956)

- The discovery of coronary angiography, which made possible the modern age of interventional cardiology and cardiovascular surgery (1958)

- Proving the viability of cadaver kidney transplants (1963)

- The first published coronary artery bypass surgery (1967)

- The discovery of a brain-mapping technique to locate the site of epileptic seizures (1970s–1980s)

- The first successful larynx transplant (1998)

- The first molecular test for thyroid cancer (2008)

- First near-total face transplant (2008)

Medical leaders at all institutions need to support intellectual curiosity, risk taking, and creativity. Like other hotbeds of innovation, Cleveland Clinic has always had a high tolerance for renegades—the kind of people who are dissatisfied with the status quo and are always looking for better ways of doing things. Because no organization can be successful unless its people are free to learn from their mistakes, Cleveland Clinic allows ample room for failure. Physicians who are driven to solve a clinical problem can, as Winston Churchill once said, go "from failure to failure without loss of enthusiasm."

One example of multiple failures that ultimately resulted in success centered on trying to find a solution to a thorny problem with blood pressure, discussed briefly in Chapter 2. Blood pressure can spike unpredictably after heart surgery, and this can lead to stroke, bleeding, disruption of vascular suture lines, and other dangerous effects. Sodium nitroprusside lowers postsurgical blood pressure effectively, but if it isn't delivered in a timely way or in the appropriate amount, it will cause the patient's blood pressure to plummet, resulting in a new set of dangers. A device that could detect a spike in the patient's blood pressure and automatically administer the correct dose of medication could solve this problem.

I discussed the idea with one of Cleveland Clinic's biomedical engineers, Dr. John Petre. Dr. Petre and I bought a personal computer (a relatively new tool in the 1980s) and developed a program that would address the drug delivery problem. It worked for exactly 15 minutes.

Then it failed.

So we went back to the drawing board and came up with another program. This time, it worked for half an hour.

Then it failed.

Our next attempt involved some significant tinkering. This time, the program worked superbly for a whole hour.

Then it failed.

It took years of late-night effort and multiple variations of the design before we had a prototype that was ready for prime time. We tested it postoperatively on 180 cardiac surgery patients in 1989 and demonstrated that it produced a substantial improvement over the manual delivery of blood pressure medication. We found a lawyer to patent the device and convinced a company to manufacture it and put together a payment program for us. One day, I walked into the CEO's office and showed him our first check. It was for $50,000, which was more than many salaries at the time. The sight of that sum alerted the organization's leaders to the fact that when medical innovations are properly managed from a business standpoint, they can support the organization's mission both clinically and economically.

The lesson here is that success can't be achieved without trying new things, and this may lead to experiencing what may even be serial failure. Failure is a fact of life, but the new ideas that ultimately come out of the process are usually worth it.

Beyond encouraging risk taking, Cleveland Clinic has communicated to our staff members that we not only tolerate but *celebrate* innovation. One way we reward innovation is with an annual $50,000 award—named in honor of Dr. F. Mason Sones—given to physicians and scientists who develop particularly notable innovations. One recent award winner is a young vascular surgeon named Dr. Roy Greenberg, whose skill set includes radiology and imaging as well as surgery.

Dr. Greenberg has focused on treating aortic aneurysms. The aorta is the largest blood vessel in the body, running from the heart to the pelvis. Disease and genetic predisposition can weaken the structural integrity of the aorta. When this happens, it can split apart in layers (aortic dissection) or swell up like a balloon (aortic aneurysm). An aortic aneurysm can burst, with fatal results. Dr. Greenberg's work may help thousands of patients with this condition avoid major surgery to save their lives.

Dr. Greenberg has been a key developer of endovascular (inside the blood vessel) stent grafting for aortic aneurysms. As noted previously, stent grafts are collapsible wire cylinders covered with synthetic fabric. They are slipped through the blood vessels to the site of an aortic aneurysm. There, the cylinders are expanded into a tubular shape and anchored to the healthy tissue above and below the diseased portion of the blood vessel. Once they are in place, the old tissue collapses around them, and they serve as sturdy new conduits for blood flow from the heart to the extremities.

The earliest versions of endovascular stent grafts were long and straight. They worked well in the straight portions of the aorta, but they could not be used in the branching, twisting segments where many aneurysms occur. Dr. Greenberg has been developing stent grafts for these harder-to-treat areas, such as the aortic arch (over the heart), the places where blood vessels branch off to the kidneys, and the place where the aorta splits to go down each leg.

Complex, branching vessels need a special kind of stent graft— one that has "windows," or little holes where the clinician can attach smaller stent grafts. Dr. Greenberg has developed windowed and branched stent grafts that can be customized to fit the individual patient's anatomy. His lab has a drawer full of these devices, which look like so many ginseng roots. These branching stent grafts are making it possible to treat aneurysms wherever they may occur, however tortuous the blood vessel. Currently, most of these branching stent grafts need to be custom-made to fit a patient's individual characteristics. But ideally, some day surgeons will be able to select from a small group of off-the-shelf models that will be adaptable to a wide range of anatomical conditions.

The current and future potential of stent grafts has implications for the cost of healthcare, the comfort of patients, and the future of surgery. The current gold standard for treating aortic aneurysms is major surgery, with the heart stopped and blood shunted through a cardiopulmonary bypass. If endovascular stent grafting can be shown to improve on the outcomes of conventional surgery, it will revolutionize the treatment of this condition and other diseases of the aortic tissue.

In the course of pursuing his vision for aortic repair, Dr. Greenberg has had to defend himself against doubters, critics, and well-informed proponents of existing treatments. As he tells it, people laughed when he first came to Cleveland Clinic and announced that his lab would work on technologies that would go into the branches of the arteries. But his program has blossomed since 2001, and he continues to evaluate new variations on endovascular aortic repair—and address new challenges.

Dr. Greenberg's endovascular stent grafts have helped lower the death rate for endovascular surgery at Cleveland Clinic from 10 to 20 percent of patients to fewer than 2 percent currently. He has greatly expanded the pool of patients who are eligible for aortic repair, as it now includes many frail or older patients who could not withstand the rigors of conventional surgery. This is not the kind of innovation that could be accomplished by a tinkerer in a basement or garage. The critical nature of the condition, the skill and experience needed to treat it, and the spectacular complexity of the surgical, radiological, and computational technology involved require the resources of a major medical center on the scale of Cleveland Clinic.

Innovation at the Margins

The physical product of Dr. Greenberg's research is mechanically simple: a tube made of wire and cloth that one can hold in the palm of one's hand. Clearly, the impact of an innovation can't be measured by the number of its moving parts. Nor is it easy to predict what will inspire an innovation. Some innovations originate from metaphorical insights and perceived similarities between seemingly unrelated processes or shapes. Dr. Willem Kolff, for example, the inventor of the kidney dialysis machine, developed a variation of his device at Cleveland Clinic that utilized an ordinary household washing machine. Years later, I invented a device used in heart valve repair that was inspired by an old-fashioned embroidery hoop.

Here's the story: In the early 1980s, surgeons repaired heart valves using either mechanical valves or valves taken from pigs. They would sew a solid ring around the outside of the valve to serve as a kind of collar. But that ring didn't move well with the physical motion of the heart as it beat.

I thought that whatever went around the mitral valve while it was being repaired should be made of a flexible material that didn't pucker when it was stitched tightly. After much trial and error, I thought of a tool used in sewing—an embroidery hoop. It's usually a round frame made of wood that holds a piece of cloth taut. The person who is sewing inserts the needle into the cloth and pulls it through, pulling the stitches tight. Then, when the hoop is removed, the result is a piece of embroidery that isn't puckered. I realized that during heart surgery, I could install a holder for a piece of cloth, put the sutures through the cloth, tie it down, and remove the holder. I would then have a flexible, measured reduction of the ring that would move as the heart beat. The product that resulted has been used in operating rooms around the world ever since. It emerged from the juxtaposition of two concepts—heart surgery and embroidery—that don't usually appear in the same sentence.

Many of my 30 patents are for ideas that were inspired by comparisons and objects outside heart surgery or that required the collaboration of professionals in other disciplines. That's where innovation happens—at the margins, where one discipline rubs up against another.

Big organizations that want to promote innovation need to increase the contacts their people have with others who are outside their narrow discipline. Thanks to the institute structure, Cleveland Clinic is now an organization in which innovation occurs naturally every day. As a result, multidisciplinary breakthroughs happen frequently.

Such was the case when the organization's top bariatric surgeon, endocrinologist, and cardiologist recently discussed one of the most pressing health issues today: diabetes. They wanted to design a high-powered study of diabetes and bariatric (weight loss) surgery. Earlier studies had shown that patients with diabetes who had bariatric surgery often saw a rapid decline in their symptoms—a much faster decline than could be explained by weight loss alone. This multidisciplinary trio compared three groups of obese patients with uncontrolled type 2 diabetes. One group was treated with optimal medical management (OMM). The next group had OMM plus gastric bypass (bariatric surgery). The last group had OMM and another kind of bariatric surgery called sleeve gastrectomy.

The results, published in the *New England Journal of Medicine*, showed that the conventional treatment improved patients' condition, but bariatric surgery combined with OMM erased the biomedical markers of diabetes in the patients studied. This was a major finding. For all practical purposes, it's a cure for diabetes. Cleveland Clinic researchers are currently enrolling patients in a second part of the study that will look at the effect of gastric bypass surgery on similar groups of patients, but this time to see how the bariatric surgery affects patients' risk of heart disease and death.

Dr. Greenberg's work on endovascular techniques is also an excellent example of collaboration across disciplines. The application of aortic stent grafting to different segments of the aorta crosses the specialties of interventional cardiology, vascular surgery, vascular medicine, and cardiac surgery. No single specialist works on this type of innovation alone. It takes a vascular surgeon, a cardiac surgeon, a cardiologist, a radiologist, and a skilled support team to make it happen. More and more specialists are working in a conceptual space where there are no historical precedents, few professional territory markers, and no status squabbles. This is the "innovation zone."

The innovation zone is not limited by time, space, or geography. The Internet provides priceless access to a world of ideas and information. But even the Internet is no substitute for "innovation trips" and safaris to strange places to encounter new ideas "in the wild." Ambitious individuals in every field need to close their laptops, get out of their chairs, and take trips to explore new places and meet people who are doing things differently—and maybe better.

I've taken about 20 innovation trips all over the world to visit other organizations and learn from their best practices. In 1996, I visited Stanford University Medical School to observe the progress it was making in heart valve surgery. At that time, valve surgery was being done through a foot-long thoracotomy, which involves cutting through the sternum and parting the ribs with a mechanical spreader to expose the heart. I came away from Stanford with the idea that it might be possible to do valve surgery through a smaller incision. I went into the lab for eight months and emerged with a new technique for minimally invasive valve surgery. To ensure that doctors everywhere could learn about this new technique, the Cleveland Clinic team did two minimally invasive valve surgeries back-to-back and broadcast them live to 4,000 surgeons in 40 cities via a worldwide video hookup.

Doctors in every specialty should take innovation trips—go to other countries, explore new technologies, visit assembly lines, and get a new perspective on their work. As CEO, I visit the World Economic Forum in Davos, Switzerland, every year. I go to learn, to network, and to share information with leaders in science, industry, and technology. During a recent trip, I spoke with top executives from two information technology powerhouses about the future of big data: how it's coming together and how we can use it to our advantage. I learned that 90 percent of all the data in the world was created in only the past two years. We talked about having a chief data officer outside the IT framework to analyze those data and put them to use. This conversation did a lot to push my thinking forward in ways that I'm sure will benefit Cleveland Clinic and how it treats patients.

Cleveland Clinic welcomes those who want to make their own innovation trip to the hospital. Every week, it's a pleasure to host executives and healthcare leaders from places such as China, India, and South America. Not long ago, a group of 60 people from Portland, Oregon, came through to learn more about the "renaissance" of Cleveland. Clinic staff members led them through the hospital's lobbies, crowded them into a catheterization lab, and showed them the extensive robotic transport system that is used to move supplies around the sprawling campus. Some of the visitors were wide-eyed. "This is all something I never expected," said one. And that's the

reason to travel: to encounter the unexpected, dismantle old prej-
udices, and return home with new perspectives on old problems.

Bringing Innovations to Market

Developing sound, workable medical technologies is only part of
the equation. The rest involves getting these inventions into the
hands of doctors across the country and around the world in something less than the current 13-year lag time between the laboratory
and the bedside.

There's already an efficient way to distribute beneficial goods
and services as quickly as possible to the people who need them:
it's called the marketplace. Commercialization provides incentives
that promote innovation and spur the rapid development of new
products. Ownership and control of a patentable idea allow the organization to set and maintain the highest quality and safety standards. Commercial enterprises can develop and deliver a product
to the very people who need it most, with unparalleled speed.

For generations, well-meaning medical pioneers have resisted
the commercial impulse. Innovators such as Dr. F. Mason Sones
and Dr. René Favaloro didn't patent their work and license it to
someone who could sell or distribute it. Cleveland Clinic could
have earned millions from the catheters that Sones designed and
another fortune from the development of the C-arm (an imaging device that wraps around a patient's gurney like the letter C).
But it just wasn't done. The organization did not have the capability to convert the innovative idea into a marketable product; that
required an outside partner in industry who could understand the
importance of the idea and was willing to risk an investment. As a
result, many innovations languished unused or undeveloped. Many
innovators saw their ideas exploited by others who were less scru-
pulous about quality and safety. And the missions of many hospitals and universities suffered from lost financial support. Cleveland
Clinic didn't file for its first patent until 1982.

Fortunately, the resistance to commercialization is dying out. To bring innovations to market, Cleveland Clinic and other academic medical centers have added technology transfer units to their organizational portfolios. These units are teams of patent lawyers, MBAs, and other experts whose function is to take charge of a doctor's or a scientist's bright idea and turn it into a product that is manufactured and sold by a viable commercial enterprise. Given the complexity of markets today, doctors need people who understand commerce in order to get medical products in front of the people who will want or benefit from them. Despite their intelligence and training, few doctors and scientists have a deep knowledge of product development, patent law, capital markets, manufacturing, or device regulation. They're not expected to. Working with the right kind of experts allows them to focus on patient care or research into the causes of and cures for disease.

Cleveland Clinic's technology transfer function, Cleveland Clinic Innovations (CCI), reviews the innovations created by the organization's 3,000 doctors and scientists; invests in them; determines whether they are commercially viable; and licenses, patents, and starts companies around those that are. CCI has subject-matter experts, executives in residence, allied investors, and business incubation specialists, plus access to investment funds and seed and technology validation funds. CCI also has the ability to arrange preclinical testing and provide access to sophisticated prototyping workshops. It's a critical mass of commercial resources focused on developing new diagnostics, software, medicines, devices, and techniques for the benefit of patients.

CCI has managed 300 patents issued over the past 10 years, and there are 1,700 more in the queue. It has spun off 55 start-ups, and nearly three-quarters of those have received equity investment—more than $650 million to date. In 2012 alone, CCI produced 38 new business licenses, 7 new spin-off companies, and 278 new invention disclosures. Companies in CCI's portfolio represent an array of technologies in the device, pharmaceuticals, and health

IT fields. These firms are actively developing technologies that will save lives and push the boundaries of medicine even further. Within Cleveland Clinic, CCI has created a community of collaborators that advances innovation in nearly every area of the organization. Caregivers across the system are discovering that innovation is an activity in which everyone—physicians, nurses, researchers, and administrators—can participate, not only a few select individuals.

CCI spin-offs include companies involved in artificial hearts, cardiac tissue regeneration, and laboratory testing of new markers for cardiovascular disease. Beyond heart-related innovations, the next important frontier in health is the brain—specifically, the treatment of neurodegenerative and movement disorders. Cleveland Clinic has a strong history in the study and treatment of multiple sclerosis (MS), a chronic disease of the nervous system for which there are few treatments and as yet no cure.

MS is a hard condition to pin down. It has multiple symptoms and severity levels, ranging from numbness in the limbs to blindness and near-total paralysis. It can affect a patient strongly at some times, while symptoms may disappear at others. It seems as if no two patients experience MS the same way.

Scientists who study MS are divided about whether it is an autoimmune disease, caused by the body's disease-fighting defense mechanisms turning on themselves, or a primary neurodegenerative disorder. Both genetic and environmental factors are believed to be involved. The disease affects about 2.1 million people around the world, about two-thirds of them women.[4]

What MS patients really need now is more knowledge about their disease and more research into effective treatments for it. Cleveland Clinic's Mellen Center for Multiple Sclerosis is at the forefront of this work. It's the largest MS treatment and research facility in the world. Some of the most important basic scientific breakthroughs involving MS in recent years, as well as studies of some of the most promising new drug therapies, have taken place at the Mellen Center. Many have involved Dr. Bruce Trapp, chair of neurosciences at Cleveland Clinic's Lerner Research Institute and a staff member at the Mellen Center.

As a pioneer in his field, Dr. Trapp has had to invent or develop many of the basic tools of MS research—methodologies that are needed to establish the groundwork for developing and testing novel therapeutics. In 2009, he and CCI launched a company, Renovo Neural Inc., to make his exclusive study techniques and methodologies available to MS researchers everywhere.

Dr. Trapp and other MS researchers know that the disease works by attacking myelin, the protective sheath that insulates microscopic nerve fibers in the brain from the environment, more or less the way a rubber sheath insulates an electric wire. MS strips the nerve fibers of myelin, disrupting the nerves' signal pathways and wreaking havoc in the person's body. So far, most treatments based on this knowledge have tried to slow or halt the progressive loss of myelin sheathing. Renovo and Dr. Trapp are taking a different approach. Their research and the research that they support are focused on restoring lost myelin—clearly a greater challenge.

Renovo's business model is to help speed the discovery of new MS drugs by providing outside researchers with the proprietary technology and techniques developed by Dr. Trapp in his extensive studies. Pharmaceutical companies that are investigating new drugs to restore lost myelin can have their compounds analyzed by Renovo to determine their ability to create new myelin sheaths in the brain. Renovo can also test the compounds using a proprietary biological model of demyelinated nerve cells. It is the only commercial entity anywhere offering these services.[5]

Renovo expanded its capabilities last year with the acquisition of a powerful new three-dimensional electron microscope (3D-EM). Previously, only universities and academic medical centers had this particular type of microscope. Independent researchers might have to wait months or years to get access to these devices. Renovo is the first company to offer access commercially. Dr. Satish Medicetty, president and CEO of Renovo, said, "With the new ease of access to 3D-EM that Renovo now provides, we believe that biological researchers will begin finding it commonplace to read tissues at the nanoscale, resulting in radically new insights—not only for basic science research, but in evaluating drugs and other therapies."[6] Dr. Trapp believes that this type of microscopy can redefine understanding of the brain and its tissues. He looks forward to its use in the effort to map all the neural connections of the brain, much as the human genome has been mapped—a field called "connectomics."

Renovo is also working on its own MS drug, which could be spun off into a separate company. For now, the business has its hands full serving its highly technical niche markets.[7]

Relying on innovations developed at Cleveland Clinic and supported by Cleveland Clinic scientific, legal, and business expertise, Renovo is poised to play an important role in the development of the next generation of MS treatments. The millions of people who have this debilitating and sometimes fatal disease are undoubtedly looking forward to the day when they can get inexpensive, effective compounds that will restore their myelin sheathing and perhaps cure MS.

Renovo is one of many companies in CCI's portfolio that have a potentially breakthrough technology. Because the goal is a much broader one of sparking a creative revolution throughout American healthcare, Cleveland Clinic doesn't stop at merely commercializing its own innovations. It brings innovators and market movers together as well. At least once a year, Cleveland Clinic becomes a gathering place for the CEOs of the nation's leading pharmaceutical and device companies, government officials, presidential cabinet members, top journalists, media figures, important legal and industrial figures, and hundreds of scientists, doctors, and inventors. They come together for the annual Medical Innovation

Summit, a three-day conclave dedicated to the discussion, dissemination, and investigation of the state of medical innovation today. Participants hear high-level presentations, debates, and disquisitions. They watch live surgeries on massive video screens, tour the facilities, and network with like minds from around the world.

CCI is also working directly with individual healthcare systems to boost those systems' innovation capabilities. While some systems are staking out new paths to technology transfer, others—such as MedStar Health, Notre Dame, Ohio State, Virginia Tech, and North Shore–Long Island Jewish Medical Center—are leveraging Cleveland Clinic's hard-earned experience. These institutions have joined a CCI program called the Healthcare Innovation Alliance, which is growing into a national network that benefits patients everywhere through joint efforts in research, clinical investigation, and the development and commercialization of new technology. Physicians across the country will be able to bring their good ideas to the market faster and more easily than ever before.

According to former CCI executive director Chris Coburn, these individual healthcare systems "frequently have many smart, high-performing doctors, but they aren't equipped institutionally to engage them around innovation." He added, "When our technology transfer company comes in and works with them, we help establish an innovation pathway by which the best new ideas can come to market. Our partner institutions experience quick jumps in the number of patents they're awarded each year." The numbers tell the story. One partner institution had no innovations on the market prior to signing up with CCI; after 15 months, more than 100 inventions had been formally presented.[8]

CCI's offices are in the Global Cardiovascular Innovation Center (GCIC), which houses a government-private consortium of the same name. GCIC is funded by the state of Ohio to promote the development of new cardiovascular treatments and devices. It is managed by Cleveland Clinic and includes local universities and medical centers in the effort to develop and launch medical technology companies. To date, GCIC has created more than 500 jobs in the companies that it funds, attracted 15 businesses to Ohio, launched and housed 25 start-up companies, awarded 52 product development grants, and secured $400 million in funding from outside investors. If more state and local governments teamed with academic medical centers in this way, the potential benefits to patients would be enormous.

Training Physician-Investigators

It's not enough to have innovative medical centers. The next generation of physicians must be trained to think more innovatively so that as they work, they can gain insight into patients' needs and strive to find new solutions. Young doctors must be educated to be curious researchers and inventors as well as knowledgeable, compassionate, and effective healers.

Doctors have talked for some time about the apparent decline in traditional physician-investigators.[9] The problem stems in part from the nature of medical education. To address these shortcomings, in 2002 Cleveland Clinic opened a new college of medicine with an ambitious goal: to reinvent medical school from top to bottom. Cleveland Clinic Lerner College of Medicine at Case Western Reserve University is strikingly different from the typical medical school. Its mission is "to educate a limited number of highly qualified persons who seek to become physician investigators and scientists committed to the advancement of biomedical research and clinical practice." The curriculum was designed by Cleveland Clinic staff physicians and includes a generous research component.

The early stages of conceptualizing the new school involved asking people throughout the organization, "How can we make this school the ideal medical education experience?" Good ideas abounded, but one that we heard repeatedly was this: "Preserve these young people from medical school debt." Many doctors graduate from medical school with hundreds of thousands of dollars in student loan debt that must be paid off before they can begin to enjoy a full income. Although many young doctors would like to pursue specialties and careers that are focused on clinical research, the need to pay down their massive amount of debt compels many of them to go into whatever specialty will make them the most money in the shortest period of time. This problem must be addressed in order to steer talented young doctors toward a research-oriented career path. Cleveland Clinic assembled a combination of institutional and donor resources and established a fund to provide full scholarships for every student admitted to the school. It's virtually free tuition.

I'll never forget the day that Norma Lerner, for whose family the school is named and whose family gift made it possible, and I stood before an assembly of students and announced the rollout of this new policy. There was an audible gasp followed by a delighted babble as students grabbed their phones to call their families and friends. It was a gratifying moment.

Although most students attend medical school for four years, students here have an additional year that is dedicated to a master's degree–level scientific research project. That in itself is not unique. But at Lerner College of Medicine, students learn about basic and translational (or clinical) research from day one, and they continue on a research track throughout their education. They are paired with both medical and research advisors to guide their progress. By the second year of their training, they participate in original scientific research projects while pursuing their clinical training.

Throughout their basic clinical education, every effort is made to foster the curiosity and inquisitiveness that great innovators commonly display. While medical education has traditionally revolved around lecturing and the rote presentation of facts, this college uses problem-based learning. Small groups of students are presented with a realistic case study of a patient showing specific symptoms. The instructor facilitates the discussions, but the students must work together to figure out what's wrong with the patient and what to do about it. Tasks are assigned that allow the students to discover the skills and knowledge that any doctor needs, both in traditional areas such as pharmacology, anatomy, and physiology and in less traditional areas such as communication and medical humanities.

Essentially, Lerner College of Medicine is training budding physicians to become lifelong learners—strong thinkers who are curious and who work proactively to satisfy their curiosity. As Dr. Kathleen Franco, associate dean of admissions, explained, "Lectures don't always engage one's mind. We want our students to ask more questions. Let me use a metaphor. We don't just want to hand them fish. We want to teach them *how* to fish."

Sometimes teachers and students go "fishing" together. Dr. Franco, who is also on the psychiatry and psychology staff at Cleveland Clinic, recalled that she was sitting in on a first-year student's research presentation when something caught her attention. "A student was presenting on epileptic seizures and the blood-brain barrier," said Dr. Franco. "The student noted that a certain protein—usually found only in the central nervous system—leaked out during seizures." (The blood-brain barrier is an organic shield that protects brain tissue from biochemical intrusion.)

Since Dr. Franco's interests include psychosis associated with epilepsy in children, she considered the student's finding in light of her own work. This set off a chain of associations that ultimately launched a new project to investigate the role of this protein in first-episode psychosis in children. She assembled a team that included the medical student, a psychiatry fellow, and staff scientists from neurosurgery and cellular and molecular medicine. The student was a full partner in the project, helping to recruit patients, draw blood, and prepare presentations. "It was a notably fruitful collaboration," said Dr. Franco. "Eight or so publications have come from the project, along with posters at international meetings. We were recently contacted by the Neuroscience Foundation to make a documentary about the role of the blood-brain barrier and inflammation in the development of psychiatric disorders in children. The foundation is even considering funding our future research."

This is a project that will ultimately help children who desperately need answers—and it all started with the findings of a first-year medical student. "This shows you how research projects can energize students, engage them in serious science, and generate the kind of questions that lead to new discoveries," said Dr. Franco.

Since the medical school is relatively new, it remains both an experiment and a work in progress. But the model is bearing fruit. Students have published important scientific papers in major journals before and after pursuing advanced training in their specialties. They have presented their research at scientific conferences across the United States. And, as predicted, a focus on research is in no way compromising the students' clinical education. It's giving them a richer, fuller appreciation of how their clinical practice fits into the larger world of scientific knowledge.

"Every day some new study results are broadcast in the national media," said Dr. Sara Lappe, a pediatrician and a graduate of Lerner College of Medicine. "Patients come in with questions based on what they've seen and read. Not all studies are created equal. I can tell at a glance which studies are strong and meaningful to my practice and which are flawed in ways that may not be noticeable to those who are not trained in science. At the same time, I may be more open to new ideas and innovative treatments because of my training." Dr. Lappe went to work at Cleveland Clinic right after her training. She's applying her research skills to the study of pediatric obesity, analyzing data on children's health from the Public Health Department.

Bright students are the rule at Lerner College of Medicine. But the brightest (so far) isn't even human. It's IBM's famous computer Watson, a version of which beat the all-time champions on the TV quiz show *Jeopardy*! That version of Watson was long ago superseded by an even more powerful Watson, the one that IBM enrolled at Lerner College of Medicine to absorb all it can about medical language, literature, and practice.

IBM is one of several companies that are working to develop computers capable of assisting doctors with diagnoses and other kinds of medical decision making. One day soon, doctors will be able to merge their intuitive understanding of patients and their problems with computer-provided insights. It's an application of big data that will dramatically enhance care. At present, Watson is very smart, but it still doesn't understand the medical context very well. So IBM asked Lerner College of Medicine to enrich and refine the big computer's decision-making capabilities.

Watson will submit data on medical problems to be corrected, recorrected, and enhanced by Lerner students and clinicians. The staff members will help Watson understand the nuances of language in the medical context. They'll make Watson a more valuable collaborator by giving it the ability to distinguish shades of meaning in what doctors say. Once Watson "graduates," it will be put to work in the clinical setting to improve and hasten decision making for the benefit of patients wherever possible.

Critics of Watson point out that a computer can be only as good as the information that's fed into it, and they question whether there is enough high-quality medical data available to give computers the medical savvy that they need. More conventional educators might also find it strange and perhaps distracting to have students learning side by side with a computer. But the staff is undeterred, and students are enthusiastic. They get to learn while they are teaching Watson. By helping it assemble evidence and chains of inference, they sharpen their own abilities to do the same. They also get to experience firsthand the cutting edge of medical innovation. Most important, they get to participate in refining an innovation—big data and big computing—that is already transforming healthcare.

When one is committed to innovation and is willing to approach medical education with an open mind and fresh eyes, the only limit is one's imagination. For a computer like Watson that wants to grow up and become a doctor and for any curious, engaged human who wants to help patients by pushing medicine further, a leading-edge medical school that does things differently is the way to go.

Looking Ahead

A willingness to innovate will determine the clinical, social, and economic future of medicine in this country. The challenge is to create an institutional architecture that supports innovation; individuals will take it from there. Innovations will succeed on their own merits. The only failure will be the stifling of innovation—the first task is to get out of the way.

Unleashing the full power of innovation will surely produce exceptional new treatments, drugs, devices, and processes for patients in the next 10 to 20 years. The most exciting advances may well be in two areas: neurological diseases and genomics. With increasing understanding of the brain, doctors are getting a better grip on diseases such as epilepsy, Parkinson's, drug addiction, and depression. And while the medicine of the past didn't take all the quirks and specificities of the human body into account, developments in genomics will allow the medicine of the future to offer vastly more effective treatments and preventive measures that are specifically tailored to each person's DNA.

The best news is that remarkable advances with respect to the diseases that afflict and frighten patients the most won't take years to accomplish. These advances are on the near horizon, and they're originating at academic medical centers such as Cleveland Clinic. One such advance pertains to breast cancer, the most frequent cause of death in women. Globally, nearly 1.5 million cases are diagnosed annually, with almost half a million deaths. Dr. Vincent Tuohy, a professor at Lerner College of Medicine and an immunology staff member at Lerner Research Institute, has been researching a breast cancer vaccine that would prevent tumors from forming. "Our research definitely represents a paradigm shift," he said. "We believe we can vaccinate people against breast cancer and other cancers the way we vaccinated them against polio."

Vaccines work by training the body's immune system to attack and destroy specific viruses or other pathogens. The problem with cancer cells is that the body produces them itself. There is no virus or other pathogen to immunize against—no single target to attack. But Dr. Tuohy is taking a different approach. He has chosen to attack what he refers to as "retired" proteins. In breast cancer, these proteins are those that enable women to lactate, an ability that ceases after a woman reaches a certain age, usually roughly 40 and certainly by menopause. He designed his vaccine to prevent these proteins from causing tumors once a woman no longer lactates.

The vaccine could also be used in younger women, especially those who they have a high risk for breast cancer. Should they become pregnant, they would need an endocrinologist to impede their ability to lactate. They would then feed their baby formula.

After quietly working on this research since 2002, Dr. Tuohy caused something of a stir in 2010 when he published a paper in *Nature* magazine describing the breast cancer vaccine for the first time. He wasn't expecting all the pushback he's received, but he realized that he was promoting a new paradigm. Dr. Tuohy is working to turn his vaccine into a product that is available to the general public. Trials with mice have succeeded, and he hopes to do Phase 1 clinical trials in humans. He is working on a similar approach to immunize women against ovarian cancer. He believes that the retired protein method can be used to develop a prostate cancer vaccine as well. "Cleveland Clinic and I have the same vision of changing the landscape of medicine," he said. "We see vaccines that prevent these cancers as an enormous missing link in healthcare."

Cures exist for polio and tuberculosis. Great strides are being made against diabetes, heart disease, and some forms of cancer. There is real hope that breast cancer might be next.

Chapter 5

Care Should Be a Healing Experience for Body and Mind

I've learned that people will forget what you said,
people will forget what you did, but people will
never forget how you made them feel.

—MAYA ANGELOU

n 2006, Harvard Business School invited me to discuss a case study on Cleveland Clinic. The first session was positive; at the second session, a student raised her hand. "Dr. Cosgrove, my father needed mitral valve surgery. We knew about Cleveland Clinic and the excellent results you have. But we decided not to go there because we heard that you had no empathy. We went to another hospital instead, even though it wasn't as highly ranked as yours."

The student then paused and looked me right in the eyes. "Dr. Cosgrove, do you teach empathy at Cleveland Clinic?"

I was floored. No one had ever asked me that before, so I didn't have much of an answer. Cleveland Clinic had recently adopted an initiative called "Patients First" that focuses on delivering better care to patients and their families. But we didn't yet *teach* empathy, and we hadn't yet committed ourselves to thinking that much about the feelings of individual patients.

Ten days after visiting Harvard, I went to Saudi Arabia for the inauguration of a new hospital. King Fahd of Saudi Arabia was there. The president of the hospital said, "This hospital is dedicated to the body, spirit, and soul of the patient." I happened to look over and saw the king weeping. Many members of the audience were crying as well.

I thought, "We're really missing something. We need to treat the soul and spirit of the patient, not just the body."

A century ago, when most doctors were solo practitioners ministering to patients, they couldn't offer sick patients many treatments that actually worked. What they could offer was reassurance, comfort, communication, and empathy. By the end of the twentieth century, however, medicine had changed. Teams of highly trained specialists had emerged, delivering complex, effective, technically advanced care. Meanwhile, the human dimension of care had fallen by the wayside. Doctors devoted most, if not all, of their energy to enhancing their ability to heal patients' bodies, not their souls. Hubris and arrogance emerged among caregivers who, ironically, had chosen their careers because they cared about patients as people and wanted to help them heal.

I was as guilty of this as anybody else. When I went to medical school in the 1960s, heart surgery was in its infancy. Up to 20 percent of patients were dying on the operating table. I focused on fine-tuning what I was doing in order to bring down the mortality rate. I didn't spend much time talking to patients or thinking about their feelings. I didn't think about society, the whole patient, or how an organization works. All I did was heart surgery—all day, every day. I spent my life in pursuit of technical excellence.

But technical excellence is not nearly enough. Doctors have always defined quality in terms of clinical outcomes—cure rates, remission rates, complication rates, mortality rates, and so on. But outcomes, which deal with the physical body, are only half the story. A galaxy of feelings and impressions is also involved in a healthcare encounter. The medical profession has a name for this: "patient experience."

Patients may not know how to measure clinical outcomes, and they may not understand the technical know-how that a doctor must have in order to perform a complex heart surgery or neurosurgery, but they can form clear judgments about their experience. They know whether their rooms are clean and whether people are polite to them. They recognize differences in the quality of the food and in how an organization looks and feels. They know whether they feel cared for. Most of all, they can tell whether they've had a healing experience—or whether being in a hospital has only impeded their healing.

Beginning in 2006, Cleveland Clinic underwent a much-needed cultural and organizational makeover. We were determined to treat the whole patient, not just the physical body, so we made the patient experience a top strategic priority. We established an Office of Patient Experience and appointed our first chief experience officer. The organization redefined "Patients First" as providing care that addresses every aspect of a patient's encounter, including both the patient's physical comfort and his educational, emotional, and spiritual needs. The goal was to create a patient experience that distinguished Cleveland Clinic from all other providers. That required making changes in two broad areas: the physical components of patient care, such as space and food; and the service-related components of patient care, including how well caregivers communicate with patients and conduct themselves as professionals.

Although room for improvement remains, patient satisfaction scores have solidly improved, and patients now write letters expressing their thanks for the way they were treated. Honest self-evaluation can be hard, but it's the only way to move forward. Now it's fulfilling to be able to tell people, "Yes, we *do* teach empathy."

Cleveland Clinic is not alone in emphasizing patient experience, but this focus is still not the norm. American healthcare must do better. In the twenty-first century, no provider can afford to offer anything less than the best clinical, physical, and emotional experience. As patients become savvier, they will increasingly judge healthcare providers not only on clinical outcomes but on their ability to show compassion and deliver excellent, patient-centered care.

The government is furthering this trend with new programs that reward the delivery of value in healthcare instead of the volume of procedures doctors perform. As part of its value orientation, the government is collecting patient satisfaction scores from hospitals around the country and disseminating them for patients to view. It is also linking Medicare reimbursement to these scores.

Medical professionals are thus feeling increasing pressure not just to talk about empathy but to take steps to demonstrate real compassion, even while lowering costs. The day is fast approaching when the profession will take to heart the words of René Favaloro, the late Cleveland Clinic surgeon who pioneered coronary artery bypass: "The patient is more than an illness. He has a soul."

Navigating the Cultural Sea Change

Cultural change is difficult for any large organization. In Cleveland Clinic's case, reorienting caregivers to provide an excellent patient experience was like teaching a bunch of right-handed people how to paint with their left hand. Surprisingly, the greatest resistance came from physicians.

Early on, Cleveland Clinic had decided to reassign the reserved parking spaces near the front of its buildings to patients, not doctors. One physician complained: "What is this, patients first and doctors last?" Exactly. Other physicians wondered whether reforms promoting kindness and compassion were necessary. They said, "Dr. Smith is kind of mean to people, but he's a great surgeon"—as if that were enough. Being a great surgeon is about both being technically proficient *and* treating patients well.

At Cleveland Clinic, we based our case for treating the whole patient on several principles, not the least of which was that it was the right thing to do. The latest research suggested that patients did better when they received more empathetic care.[1] To drive this point home, skeptics were asked to put themselves in the patient's shoes. What if they were lying in that bed? How would they want to be treated?

Cleveland Clinic also reiterated the business case for change. Because current technology can level the playing field with respect to the outcomes that patients might receive at competing hospitals, Cleveland Clinic could further differentiate ourselves by treating patients well and providing a true healing experience. A speaker at a recent Patient Experience Summit put it well: medical centers, like all businesses, "need customers more than customers need [them]."[2]

When the government decided to emphasize patient experience, Cleveland Clinic reminded skeptics that we could choose to change because it was the right thing to do or because the government said it was the right thing to do. Regardless of the impetus, treating the whole patient has become central to Cleveland Clinic's mission.

Within the first couple of years after that encounter at Harvard Business School, Cleveland Clinic made a number of initial changes that demonstrated that our commitment to putting patients first was more than just talk. We made medical records more accessible so that patients could view them whenever they liked and informed patients that they had a right to do so. We did away with that longtime irritant, visiting hours. Recognizing how important family members are to the healing process, caregivers began encouraging them to visit whenever they liked and to spend as much time as possible (with the exception of the intensive care unit, where families might have to stay in the waiting room when caregivers are working with the patient). A multidisciplinary team enlisted fashion designer Diane von Furstenberg to help create an alternative to the traditional open-back gown to address the frequent patient complaints about the indignity and discomfort they suffered when wearing those gowns. These policy changes and initiatives might seem minor, but they have made a big difference.

As another example of putting patients first, Cleveland Clinic expanded our "redcoats" program. Redcoats are greeters in red coats whose sole job is to orient patients, provide directions, get them wheelchairs—whatever needs to be done. "It is very overwhelming coming here," says redcoat Jeannie Parish. "Sometimes patients come by themselves from far away, and then they are told that they have a terrible disease. They have to find their way back to their car. We intercede for them in any way we can. Maybe they need a sandwich or a glass of water or a shoulder to cry on or a hug. We want to make sure that people never leave here being upset with the care they received. We want them to know that someone cares."

Cleveland Clinic has also made ongoing efforts to improve the look and feel of our physical space. Many medical environments seem sterile, institutional, and impersonal—not the best places to heal. Along with decluttering and sprucing up our existing hospitals, Cleveland Clinic made our new facilities feel homier by making them more open, better organized, and bathed in natural light. All facilities implemented more comforts for families, such as pull-out beds in some of the rooms. On the main campus, a rooftop terrace was built to provide patients and their families with a soothing place outdoors, away from the hospital's clinical atmosphere.

We also improved our food, making it healthier and more appetizing, and introduced a medical concierge to provide assistance to patients traveling from out of state. We rolled out Cleveland Clinic Caring Canines, certified therapy dogs and volunteer handlers who provide emotional support, increase the number of smiles, and generally reduce anxiety for patients and their families. And the list goes on.

These changes were conceived in response to patient feedback and caregivers' intuitive sense of what was wrong with the typical hospital experience. Patients' ratings of Cleveland Clinic on government-mandated satisfaction surveys help the organization monitor our progress. Survey results are compiled into dashboards, categorized by hospital, department, and unit, which are used to continually improve and tweak our operations.

To identify areas of improvement, the Office of Patient Experience collaborates with the Institute Experience Council, a group of doctors and nurses from each institute and from Cleveland Clinic's community hospitals and health centers. Within each hospital unit, patient experience teams comprising doctors, nurses, housekeepers, and other personnel meet regularly to review patient surveys and address negative comments.

Patients have a say, too. The Office of Patient Experience organized more than 15 Voice of the Patient Advisory Councils, which are made up of current and former patients who meet regularly to discuss issues affecting patients and their families. They review new policies affecting patient experience and advise the organization on educational materials and environmental changes.

In addition, the Market Research Department formed an online panel of more than 4,000 patients and contacted panel members once or twice a month to ask questions about patient experience issues and get creative ideas. One patient wrote, "This program makes me feel like I help in some of the decisions that are made at Cleveland Clinic." Another wrote, "It makes me feel that you actually care about patients and their concerns."

The process for improving patient experience led to the creation of many new programs. For instance, the staff began using green cleaning products that were safer for the environment, patients, and caregivers. And an innovative initiative called HUSH

(Help Us Support Healing) outlined specific measures to reduce the noise commonly found in hospitals. From 9 p.m. to 7 a.m., lights are dimmed, patients' doors are closed, overhead paging is eliminated, phones and pagers are placed on vibrate, patients are offered earplugs and eye masks, TVs are used with headsets, and caregivers and visitors are asked to hold conversations in a quiet and respectful manner.

Ultimately, all these changes have stemmed from the desire and determination to empathize with patients—to understand and respect how they *feel*—in addition to providing them with the best medical care. They reflect the creed articulated by one of Cleveland Clinic's founders, Dr. William Lower, who wrote in the 1920s that "a patient is the most important person in the institution" and is not a statistic.

Patient-Centered Care
Calls for All Hands on Deck

Patrice "Peaches" Houston interacts with patients all day long. Her job is to help transport patients to and from hospital rooms and appointments, using a golf cart. In January 2010, NPR *Weekend Edition* reporter Scott Simon had a chance to meet Peaches when he came to Cleveland Clinic for care. He tweeted to his 1.3 million followers about how she made his family's experience something to remember. His message read: "Excellence of docs and researchers at Cleveland Clinic well-known, but we've also been impressed by: lab techs, floor staff and Peaches—who drives the cart between buildings. They have filled an anxious time for our family with laughter and warmth."

Peaches reported that after their stay, Simon's two young daughters sent her flowers with a thank you letter expressing how glad they were to have gotten to know her. "I often get to know families in this job. Everybody, especially the kids, loves to ride in the cart. I like helping people. It's the people that keep me going. I know this person is sick, and I do or say whatever I can to put a smile on her face."

Cleveland Clinic is privileged to have many devoted caregivers like Peaches Houston. One nurse helped a seriously ill teenage girl walk down the hall to meet another girl her age. As the mother of the first girl said, this encounter "helped [our daughter] see her own situation in an entirely new and compassionate [way]. I think the girls will be friends forever." A doctor on staff impressed a patient by thanking him for the privilege of taking care of him. As this patient recalled, "I tried to think of when a physician last expressed *and* acted on these words to me." One receptionist similarly dazzled a third patient by making an extra effort to get him an echocardiogram in time for him to return to work after his lunch hour. Still another person wrote to express his appreciation for the registered nurse who delivered his stillborn baby with great compassion, taking time to grieve with him and his wife and letting them say goodbye.[3]

The core of a better patient experience isn't better gowns or changes in visiting hours or cleaner rooms (although all these are important). It's improving how people at Cleveland Clinic treat others that they encounter, one patient and one moment at a time. Government-mandated surveys ask patients questions about the interpersonal treatment they've received: What attitude did hospital staff members show your visitors? How friendly was your doctor, and how much time did she spend with you? Did hospital staff members address your emotional needs? Cleveland Clinic wants to give its patients good reason to provide glowing responses.

"Our goal is to avoid the dispassionate and cold care that patients used to receive at our hospitals and probably at most hospitals," said Dr. James Merlino, our current chief experience officer. "We want our people to be empathetic caregivers who take the time to treat people well. We may not have the hard data to prove it, but we believe in our hearts that a patient who is treated with warmth and respect will get better faster."

This isn't a merely academic topic. Doctors are patients, too— and some of them have had sick family members who haven't received the most compassionate treatment. Dr. Merlino thought he would never work at Cleveland Clinic after his father was treated there and died of a complication. Our future chief experience officer considered the medical care excellent, but was less impressed by the patient experience. "I'm sure my father died thinking that Cleveland Clinic was the worst possible place. The nurses didn't respond when he called. When he asked for something, it didn't come. The staff members didn't seem to get along very well with one another. It was terrible. So we've been determined to change all that. We know we can do better and bring out our most compassionate selves on the job. It's an initiative that means everything to me, both professionally and personally."

What was required to change the everyday behavior of 43,000 care providers? At Cleveland Clinic, it involved inculcating a strong service mentality. Dr. Merlino told of a time in 2009 when he spotted a spill on the floor outside one of the elevator banks. He walked to the cafeteria to get paper towels to clean it up. As he returned, he saw a number of other employees walking over the spill, completely ignoring it. It struck him that they weren't engaged enough in the organization's mission to protect visitors who might slip on the spill and fall. That wasn't good enough.

To ensure that patients are treated more humanely and respectfully, Cleveland Clinic has had to foster a culture in which everyone takes ownership—a culture in which people connect everything they do, whether or not it is related to their specific job, to the organization's mission of caring for and empathizing with patients. So, regardless of whether they are surgeons, nurses, administrators, or other staff members, if they come across a spill, they clean it up. If visitors ask where the bathroom is or appear lost, they offer to help them find their way. And if, like Peaches Houston, they encounter a patient or visitor who is having a rough day, they offer comfort with a kind word or gesture.

Cleveland Clinic surveyed our caregivers to measure how engaged they were with their jobs and held managers accountable for improving engagement. We invested millions of dollars in training caregivers to understand the organization's mission and how they fit in, with the goal of ensuring that *everyone* who comes in contact with patients, not just doctors, sees himself as a care provider.

In 2011, all 43,000 caregivers went offline for a day to attend Cleveland Clinic Experience sessions called "Communicate with H.E.A.R.T." (Hear, Empathize, Apologize, Respond, Thank). Each session included pep talks and training. Videos of patient stories reminded everyone of why she had gone into healthcare to begin with. But the real work of the day took place at the tables, where caregivers from every level of the organization mingled (for example, the chief financial officer sat with a perfusionist, a surgeon, a lab tech, and a housekeeper). They shared stories, complaints, and ideas and talked about how they could make their jobs better and make the organization a better place for caregivers and patients alike. At the end of the session, everyone received a badge that identified him as a "caregiver."

As of this writing, every new caregiver who is hired, regardless of position or pay grade, receives this training. Cleveland Clinic has copyrighted the training materials and shared them with several other medical institutions that were interested in improving how their own employees think about their roles. Recognizing that a day of training is not enough to change behavior permanently, the organization has created a number of other training modules that emphasize strong communication skills and service-related behaviors.

"Respond with H.E.A.R.T." teaches all caregivers how to address patients' concerns consistently and well when problems arise. "Shop for H.E.A.R.T." trains caregivers to watch their peers and hold them accountable for providing excellent patient service. "S.T.A.R.T. with Heart" lets caregivers practice identifying emotions and expressing empathy. And "Lead with H.E.A.R.T." gives managers and supervisors techniques that they can use in every interaction with their teams and with patients and visitors in order to create an ideal service culture.

All evidence suggests that this training is working. Since 2008, employee engagement scores have trended consistently upward, as have patient ratings of their experience. The number of patient complaints has declined. And every week, Cleveland Clinic receives letters from patients describing how meaningful and helpful their interactions with individual caregivers have been.

Improving Caregiver-Patient Communication

Helping all employees see themselves as caregivers was an important step forward, but it wasn't enough. Members of a medical staff can be extremely engaged in their jobs and the mission of the organization without necessarily projecting the desired level of empathy. Why? Because they don't know how to communicate with patients. Efforts at improving patient experience aren't worth anything without strong caregiver-patient communication. Such communication encourages patients to comply with their doctor's advice and to take their medications, improving health outcomes while reducing patient anxiety. In addition, physicians who listen and show respect are less likely to be sued, so they need to be very attentive to communication.

Cleveland Clinic assembled a panel of more than 70 physicians from inside and outside the organization to help produce a physician guide to patient-centered communication. The guide contains the basic standards drawn up for the medical community by the Institute of Medicine and the American Medical Association, along with detailed conversation tips and strategies for dealing with difficult patients. The guide applies equally to residents and fellows, since they too need to be well versed in interpersonal skills. To help them master the art of interacting with patients, trainees receive conversation tips and guidelines on cards that fit easily into the pocket of a lab coat.

In recognizing the importance of the patient's frame of reference in caregiver-patient communications, Cleveland Clinic makes a concerted effort to educate patients and encourage them to partner with their providers in their care. Each inpatient receives a brochure titled "What to Expect During Your Hospital Stay," which explains the many kinds of professionals that patients might encounter during their stay and advises patients about what to expect regarding medications, the hospital environment, and the discharge process. It also encourages patients to ask questions and jot down concerns as they arise. "Patients need to bear some of the responsibility for good communication," Dr. Merlino says. "They can help by knowing what to expect and telling us what's working and what isn't."

Cleveland Clinic has introduced patient service navigators (PSNs) to assist with communication between patients and caregivers. PSNs are patient advocates who help address patient and family needs. They visit patients daily and provide personalized guidance and support, orienting new patients to the services and daily schedules in a hospital unit and sharing information about the healthcare team. PSNs also tell family members what they need to know about parking, lodging, cafeterias, and other services, and they are available to help resolve conflicts between patients and caregivers.

PSNs can make all the difference between an ordinary experience and an extraordinary one. For example, one PSN worked with nurses to help a terminally ill patient attend his daughter's wedding by arranging to have the wedding right in the patient's nursing unit. Food, flowers, and parking passes were donated, and a social worker and the patient's oncologist performed readings. The family was grateful that the patient had the opportunity to participate in his daughter's special day.

Good communication transcends conversation and extends to the environment and the overall institution. Cleveland Clinic redesigned the signs in its halls to make them easier to follow and also changed caregivers' uniforms. Patients had said that they found it hard to know what was happening when all sorts of caregivers were running in and out of their room performing tests, cleaning, checking their charts, and so on. Consequently, Cleveland Clinic decided that from then on, all nurses would wear white, doctors would wear white lab coats, lab technicians would wear red scrubs, nursing assistants would wear green scrubs, and so on. Patients receive a brochure that identifies these colors. The mandate wasn't exactly popular among nurses; they were used to wearing their favorite-colored scrubs and didn't want to wear plain white. But since it helped the institution become more intelligible to patients, it was yet another way to put patients first.

Cleveland Clinic also trains our medical students to become better communicators and more empathetic in general. At least one study has shown that physicians in training become *less* empathetic as they go through medical school.[4] That's understandable, given the intensely competitive guild-style training that medical students typically receive. The long hours and other pressures of postgraduate training and working as a doctor can take their toll. Cleveland Clinic's Lerner College of Medicine has incorporated training in the humanities in order to teach professionalism and communication. Scholarly presentations help students and residents reflect on various aspects of medicine, the patient as a person, their growth as physicians and as individuals, and healthcare delivery in general.

A student at the college participated in a performance of dramatic vignettes based on reflective writing that he and other first-year students had done. As he reported, "I reflected after anatomy lab that our medical training held the risk of our seeing patients as bodies, not as people. When we came together and watched a dramatization of our experiences, it opened up a dialogue with the person inside the body, with the unspoken thoughts and feelings of my classmates, and with my own fears and awakenings."

Dr. James Young, dean of the medical school, used an apt metaphor to describe the college's goals for the training: "We were trying to blow on those embers of empathy that are present in everyone and get them burning at the appropriate level. We were teaching students to recognize the challenges to empathy that they're likely to encounter while practicing medicine and to develop techniques to take care of themselves—have empathy for themselves—so that they can be there fully for others."

Communicating better is an ongoing effort. To track how well caregivers are pleasing patients, senior leaders make rounds through the hospital on a monthly basis. In 2013, I was making one of these rounds when I visited a Vietnam veteran who was African American. When I inquired about his experience, he said that everything was great. But something about the way he said it suggested that there was an issue. "Are you sure there's nothing we can improve?" I asked.

The man thought for a moment. "Well, there's one thing. People around here should learn how to address other people in a respectful manner."

I didn't know what he meant, so I asked him to elaborate.

"Well, one of the nursing assistants comes in every day, and I'm sure she doesn't understand what she's saying, but she calls me 'sunshine.' I'm from the South, and in the South, slaves were called 'sunshine.' It's a derogatory term for black males. I'm a veteran; people should show more respect."

He was right—the nursing assistant had no idea that she was causing offense. Upon hearing what the patient had said, she burst into tears at the thought that her innocent words had been misconstrued. To avoid similar problems, Cleveland Clinic enacted a service standard directing all caregivers not to call people by familiar terms such as "honey," "dear," or "sunshine." Unless patients give permission to call them something else, caregivers need to use "Mr.," "Mrs.," "Ms.," or "Miss."

The Ritz-Carlton Hotel Company famously describes its mission as "ladies and gentlemen serving ladies and gentlemen." Cleveland Clinic wanted to provide that same level of respect and decorum and make our communications more satisfying for patients. They deserve nothing less.

CALL TODAY FOR AN APPOINTMENT TODAY

It's a funny thing about patients. They get so *im*patient—and for good reason. When you're sick, you don't want to wait for medical care. You want it now. We understand. Cleveland Clinic gives anyone who calls before noon a very special option— the same-day appointment.

We believe that every life deserves world-class care today. Not a month from now.

Cleveland Clinics' leaders launched the push for same-day appointments six years ago. Multidisciplinary teams were formed. Procedures and processes were analyzed. Roadblocks were cleared, and the first same-day patients started streaming in.

"We applied advanced industrial efficiency techniques to the challenge of making same-day appointments," says Dr.

Tree of Life

In 2007, Cleveland Clinic installed a piece by artist Jennifer Steinkamp on its main campus. Titled *Mike Kelley* after Steinkamp's mentor, the work is a constantly moving video installation of a tree. Not just any tree—a fantastical, glowing, fluorescent tree that changes with the seasons. The tree transfixes patients and visitors alike. Some of them have asked, "How can I get one of those?" Little children run up to the white wall on which the tree is projected, trying to touch the leaves and hug the tree trunk. In fact, people approach the wall so often that it has had to be repainted several times to keep it white. Responding to patient requests, Cleveland Clinic installed a bench nearby so that patients and visitors could sit and

A. Marc Harrison, who was chief medical operations officer during the implementation of same-day appointments (he's now CEO of Cleveland Clinic Abu Dhabi). "Everyone was focused on one goal: to make getting into Cleveland Clinic fast, easy, and friendly."

How does it work? You need to call before noon. You will be asked some questions. Based on your answers, you will be given the choice of seeing whatever doctors or nurse-practitioners are appropriate to your needs and are available at whichever Cleveland Clinic facility has an opening on the same day. If you call between noon and 5 p.m., you can get a next-day appointment.

"Same-day patients may be seen at our main campus, family health centers, or community hospitals," says Dr. Cynthia Deyling, chair of regional operations. "We believe we are the only major medical center in America to offer same-day appointments."

watch the tree sway. Caregivers, too, found it rejuvenating to spend time by the tree after a long day.

One day in early 2013, Joanne Cohen, executive director of Cleveland Clinic's art program, was strolling by the tree with some colleagues. A mother was taking photos of her teenage daughter in front of the work. "Would you like us to take a picture of the two of you together?" Cohen and her colleagues asked.

"No," the mother replied. "I just want to take pictures of my daughter. It's a tradition. We do it every year."

Joanne was curious and asked the mother for her family's story.

"You know," she said, "my daughter had a very serious health problem a few years ago. She was airlifted here. Thankfully, she got better, and so every year when we come back for her annual checkup, we take a picture of her in front of the tree. It's something we look forward to."

In 2013, the Jennifer Steinkamp tree was just one of approximately 5,000 pieces of primarily museum-quality art displayed on the 23 million square feet of wall space in Cleveland Clinic's network. As part of its strategy to improve patient experience, the organization has invested millions since 2006 in upgrading the art on our facility walls. The goal is to enhance, enliven, and inspire patients, caregivers, and the community—and ultimately, to make the spaces more inviting and uplifting. The collection includes contemporary art by local, national, and international artists. As at a museum, educational wall labels describe the artists and the works, making them accessible. Family members who might be spending days on end with a loved one can pass the time by taking an audio tour of 35 works in the collection. In addition, an exhibition space features shows that rotate every three or four months.

Many hospitals have art on the walls, but they don't tend to put a lot of money, thought, or effort into it. The works displayed tend to be pretty landscapes that don't demand much of viewers. Cleveland Clinic deliberately chooses to push the boundaries of what might be appropriate to show in a hospital. Some of the works are quite challenging, dealing with difficult subjects or violating accepted notions of what is beautiful. As Cohen explained, "We're trying to make the hospital experience feel like something else. And we're trying to make viewers feel something. Why can't you experience serious, provocative art in a hospital context? Why does all hospital art have to be pretty and comforting? We like our art to do what the best art does—expand our perspectives, take us outside ourselves, and allow our imaginations to soar beyond the problems we might currently be facing."

Hardly a week goes by without patients saying how meaningful and healing the art has been. "I could hardly walk down any main hallway without stopping the first time I was there," one of them wrote. The art "is very compelling and somehow distracts me from the real reason for being here. Good art . . . draws me into the universality of the human condition and makes every aspect of it acceptable somehow—and you don't have to be able to verbalize what art is or even your opinion about it to feel it. It is a feeling that stays with you."

Another patient, a priest, was so captivated by the "beautiful, challenging, and depth-eliciting art" that he offered a painting of his own as a gift for others to enjoy. He also wrote that the artworks "touch the spirit—healing it and, I suspect, the body as well."

A 2012 survey found that Cleveland Clinic's art collection had measurable effects on patients' moods, comfort, stress, and overall impression of the hospital. Almost three-quarters of respondents said that the art put them in a better mood. Patients with PTSD (posttraumatic stress disorder), generalized anxiety, and breast cancer were most likely to say that their mood, comfort level, and stress level had improved. And almost 80 percent of all respondents said that the art enhanced their impression of Cleveland Clinic.

The art program is just one of many ways in which Cleveland Clinic incorporates spirituality into healing through our Arts & Medicine Institute. Another vehicle is music; hundreds of musical performances for patients, visitors, and members of the community take place on-site each year. Extensive music therapy programs allow patients to listen to music as part of their healing. "Music therapy is a place where [patients] can feel safe, comfortable, and in the driver's seat," said Mia Roberge, a former Cleveland Clinic music therapist. "If the patient goes from maybe having a little bit of a frown or their body is tense to relaxing or smiling, or if I help to bring their pulse down or their heart rate is a little bit better, I've done my job."

Many studies have confirmed that art and music therapy can help ease pain and suffering for seriously ill patients. "We've found that we can do many things with music," says Maria Jukic, executive director at the Arts & Medicine Institute. "We can improve the gait of someone with multiple sclerosis and improve a patient's speech after a stroke. Because it touches the social, spiritual, and emotional sides of healing, music is extremely powerful."

Emotional Healing

As a scientific organization, Cleveland Clinic must draw a sharp line between activities that have a physical or scientific basis and those whose mechanisms are more subjective. But some emotional conditions may benefit most from a mix of objective and subjective therapies. A hospital is a unique environment that encompasses the extremes of human experience: birth, death, hunger, pain, loss, anxiety, longing, parting, relief, elation, and spiritual renewal. Many patients, visitors, and caregivers would prefer not to experience these states alone; many of them yearn for guidance, focus, or someone to talk with or to listen to them.

The Reverend Dennis Kenny, director of spiritual care at Cleveland Clinic, knows the full range of emotions that can be experienced in the healthcare setting. He and his colleagues in the Center for Ethics, Humanities and Spiritual Care established the Department of Healing Services to address the multiplicity of emotional and spiritual conditions for which patients may want and need attention. Healing Services can arrive at the patient's bedside in many forms; the team includes social workers, specially trained nurses, chaplains, and massage therapists and offers relaxation techniques such as guided imagery, meditation, hypnotherapy, and touch therapies. Many of these services are offered at no charge. They overlap with treatments offered through the Center for Integrative Medicine (which also offers acupuncture, mind/body coaching, chiropractic and holistic psychotherapy, and specialized weight-loss programs).

Patients, visitors, or caregivers who feel an urgent need for this kind of attention can call on the services of the Code Lavender team, named with a color, as are other urgent hospital calls. Summoned to the scene of an emotional emergency, the Code Lavender team can provide immediate comfort, counseling, and therapies or services that extend across two or three days.

When Reverend Kenny and his colleagues launched the Code Lavender team, they anticipated an equal number of calls from patients, visitors, and patient care personnel. To their surprise, 95 percent of calls come from caregivers. Perhaps this shouldn't have been so unexpected. Hospital caregivers are highly trained professionals, but they are also human beings with emotions, memories, and experiences that affect their responses to illness and mortality, just as they affect anyone else's. In forming personal bonds with the patients and families that they serve, they may feel a strong individual stake in the outcome of a patient's treatment or care. Caregivers do not get used to death and suffering; instead, they develop strategies that enable them to function amid these profound moments. Healing Services is able to give these caregivers the kind of immediate support that they sometimes need.

Natoma's Story

In 2010, Natoma Canfield, a middle-aged woman from Medina, Ohio, took a bold step and wrote a letter to President Barack Obama that described her inability to afford medical coverage. The letter went viral, becoming a focal point for public discussion and debate. Two months later, Natoma started feeling tired and sick. One day, she collapsed and was taken to a Cleveland Clinic hospital. She was near death and needed immediate blood transfusions.

The next day, she was diagnosed with leukemia, and her worst fear had come to pass: having a serious illness, yet lacking insurance to fall back on. She had the worst kind of leukemia and required a bone marrow transplant. Even with that extreme measure, she stood only a 33 percent chance of recovering.

Natoma was eligible for several types of government and private assistance. Cleveland Clinic provided charity care based on her income and helped her receive government assistance through

Medicaid and Medicare. Over the next nine months, Natoma underwent an extreme regimen that included chemotherapy and radiation. For many days, she lay in bed, unable to do anything; her head was so scattered from the treatments that she could barely recite the alphabet. She was afraid that she would never be able to think normally again or perform everyday activities.

Encouraged by her doctors, she had the bone marrow transplant. She waited for the levels of platelets in her blood to go up. The doctors tried drugs and other treatments, to no clear effect. "And then one day," Natoma's sister tearfully recalled, "they started going up. And they kept going up."

As of 2013, Natoma's platelet levels are almost normal, and she is back home, able to embrace life again. Natoma and her family don't just credit the treatments themselves for enabling her to beat her life-threatening disease. "The doctors and nurses, we can't say enough about the good treatment they provided," her sister related. "And not just them. It's everyone. It's the whole philosophy, the things that aren't medical that make a patient come back. The cleaning lady who comes in and is so positive. The social workers. The cafeteria workers. The valets that helped us. The redcoats. The yoga instructor who helped us forget about leukemia for an hour. The appointment ladies who always treated my sister with dignity and respect. Sometimes it's just the person who smiles or hugs you. When you live at a hospital for two years, it's wonderful that you have those resources. These are the kinds of things that you just don't ever forget."

Natoma recalled an episode with the music therapist that was critical to her recovery. "A woman comes around. She has a little piano and guitar, and we sang songs together. That was the beginning of my healing experience."

What Natoma experienced was a new kind of hospital—one that didn't just offer the technically excellent care that she needed, but that attended to her soul and her spirit as well. Every patient, at every hospital, should experience care like this; it helps to improve patient outcomes and is a less costly way of delivering care. The medical profession seems to be getting the message and moving toward a more humane, compassionate, and enriching patient experience.

But we need to speed up the pace. You can help by paying attention to how your doctors communicate and to the general atmosphere of your local hospitals. Look up patient satisfaction scores on the Internet. If you're not satisfied with the care you're receiving, say something. Make an effort to understand your condition and to ask your doctor questions. Be an active partner in the care you're receiving.

Putting patients first is better for both patients and caregivers. For caregivers, it makes the practice of medicine much more fulfilling. One patient wrote that there were "no words to describe this place called Cleveland Clinic." As this patient told us, "In the film *Field of Dreams*, Shoeless Joe Jackson walks to the edge of the ball field and asks Kevin Costner's character, 'Is this heaven?' Costner's character answers, 'No, it's Iowa.' For us, the answer is, 'No, it's Cleveland,' a line we are unable to say without tears welling in our eyes."

Wellness Depends on Healthcare, Not Sick Care

Although doctors are in the healthcare business, they spend most of their time caring for patients who are anything but healthy. What if, instead of working to make sick people healthy, Cleveland Clinic concentrated on keeping them healthy to begin with? What if it took the lead in moving America and the medical profession away from "sick care" and toward true healthcare? Don't healthcare organizations have a responsibility to demonstrate what healthy behavior is?

America is seeing an epidemic of chronic illness—not just heart disease but cancer, diabetes, hypertension, emphysema, and a number of other conditions. These diseases are now so prevalent and so costly that they're threatening to destroy America's broader economic health. The country is at a turning point, and if people don't develop healthier habits, the damage will be permanent.

There's still hope. Individuals *can* prevent themselves from getting sick in the first place, but this country needs a new cultural paradigm—one that promotes healthy lifestyles, discourages bad habits, and supports people in making and sustaining healthy changes. And medical institutions need to lead the way, not only by encouraging patients along these lines, but also by first changing the culture within the institution.

Cleveland Clinic has been doing our part since 2004. Tens of thousands of Cleveland Clinic caregivers have stopped smoking, lost weight, developed new exercise routines, and gained better control of their chronic diseases. They've been encouraged by a new culture that focuses on the principles of wellness. The most celebrated change has been the in-house financial incentives offered to caregivers to stay in shape and manage their chronic illnesses. If they make healthier lifestyle choices, they can potentially save hundreds of dollars on their health insurance each year. These incentives have saved Cleveland Clinic more than $15 million in healthcare costs and improved the lives of thousands of caregivers and their families.

Improved wellness is an ongoing journey, but the strides that the institution has made along that path are significant and include the following:

- Committing to wellness
- Banning smoking on all Cleveland Clinic properties
- Hiring only nonsmokers
- Providing financial incentives for caregivers to quit smoking, lose weight, eat better, and manage their chronic diseases
- Creating a Wellness Institute led by a chief wellness officer
- Partnering with government and the community to spread the wellness word outside the organization
- Removing sugared drinks and trans fats from the cafeterias and vending machines
- Offering free Weight Watchers and gym memberships

As of 2013, the institution has implemented more than 80 policies and programs aimed at wellness and is seeing many of the benefits that it had anticipated—not just significant cost savings but happier, more engaged caregivers and patients.

Large health organizations can make huge strides by embracing wellness, and they can help their surrounding communities get healthier. If everyone—individuals, medical institutions, business, and government—were to take a proactive stance on healthcare and embark on wellness journeys of their own, the United States could radically improve the welfare of individuals and society alike. Americans can avoid the decay of their living standards and enjoy longer, healthier, happier lives.

Bad Habits Cost More Than Money

Do poor habits such as smoking or eating too much unhealthy food really pose a dire public health problem? The facts tell the story. Despite widespread antismoking campaigns, about a fifth of Americans still smoke, and some 4,000 people under the age of 18 try their first cigarette each day.[1]

Only 13 percent of American men and 9 percent of American women report that they exercise vigorously for 10 minutes or more five or more times a week. The vast majority of Americans never break a sweat. Most Americans eat the wrong foods—and too much of them. All this is leading to an epidemic of obesity.

According to the National Institutes of Health, some 63 million Americans now qualify as obese, defined as having a body mass index (BMI) of 30 or more (BMI is calculated as a function of height and weight).[2] Of these, 3 million are described as being superobese, or 100 pounds or more above their normal weight. Obesity, like smoking, is taking a severe toll on the American population. The Centers for Disease Control and Prevention identifies tobacco use, poor diet, physical inactivity, and alcohol abuse as the leading factors in American death statistics. Infections and viruses, by contrast, are way down the list.

It's true that deaths from heart disease have decreased—from 203 per 100,000 people in 1979 to 135 per 100,000 people today. This reduction has resulted from improved treatments, preventive care, and heightened awareness of the major risk factors, such as smoking, inadequate exercise, and eating the wrong foods. Yet heart disease remains the leading cause of death among men and women, affecting 16.8 million Americans.

The American Heart Association estimates that about every 34 seconds, an American will have a heart attack. In addition, the lifetime risk of having cardiovascular disease after age 40 is two in three for men and more than one in two for women. Meanwhile, rates of other chronic illnesses remain high or are trending upward. Rates of diabetes have more than quadrupled since 1990, with growing numbers of young children developing this chronic condition. Obesity may be responsible for up to a quarter of some of the most common and deadly cancers, including gallbladder, ovarian, and pancreatic cancer.

The human toll that these diseases are taking is obvious, but the economic and societal burden is severe, too. Healthcare costs are skyrocketing, and chronic illness is the culprit—not insurers, doctors, the government, or drug companies. Behavior-related factors, including tobacco use, poor food choices, excessive portion sizes, and physical inactivity, now account for 75 percent of all healthcare costs. Preventable chronic diseases are responsible for 81 percent of all hospital admissions in the United States, 91 percent of all prescriptions, and 76 percent of all physician visits. All this adds up to an average annual healthcare cost of $6,000 for every American citizen.

The state of a nation's economy is only as good as the state of its citizens' health. Because of preventable chronic diseases, America spends twice as much on healthcare as Europe and Canada do and four times as much as Mexico, Japan, and India. The United States also has 80 percent more high blood pressure, 110 percent more heart disease, 40 percent more diabetes, and 800 percent more strokes than other developed countries.

In 2011, 17.9 percent of gross domestic product (GDP) was spent on healthcare,[3] and that number is projected to increase. According to Congressional Budget Office figures, federal expenditures for everything but healthcare will decline as a percentage of GDP over the next 70 years. Without new sources of funding, the United States won't be able to spend as much on defense or education because it's paying to care for people who are needlessly sick. Healthcare will be rationed too, even beyond the medicines that are already rationed. America's economic competitiveness will suffer, resulting in a decline in the service industries and the loss of millions of jobs. Future generations of Americans will not live as long or enjoy the same level of prosperity as their parents did.

There is a potential upside: Americans have everything they need to save themselves and their country. If they were to spend less than 18 or 19 percent of GDP on healthcare, the savings could be devoted to social problems, education, defense, and other areas that they care about. Such a scenario is possible, but as noted earlier, it requires a cultural paradigm shift—away from treating sickness and disease and toward preventing them and promoting and sustaining a culture of wellness.

As bestselling author Dr. Michael Roizen, Cleveland Clinic's chief wellness officer (and the first such officer in the United States), likes to point out, people who stop smoking before age 35 can live just as long as someone who never smoked. Regular exercise in middle to late life decreases the risk of heart attack by 55 percent, the risk of dying of cancer by 45 percent, and the risk of dying of infection by 95 percent. The overall death rate drops 60 percent. Studies have shown that even people in their eighties see a benefit.

Despite the commonly held notion that both the body and the mind begin their downhill slide after age 30, the facts tell a different story. An ongoing study of Harvard physicians begun in the 1950s found that the IQ of these doctors declined over time by about 5 percent for every 10 years of life. This finding wasn't unexpected, but the study discovered something else: despite the overall decline, some participants—about a quarter of them—*didn't* see their IQs decline as they aged. And this was true of other measures of health, such as bone density, muscle mass, heart function, and lung function.

Some people may see their bodies decline very little (if at all) over time. The key is how well they take care of themselves. Before 35 years of age, genes largely account for a person's overall health. After 35, a person's health is mainly within her control. Unfortunately, too many Americans take the fast slide to an early death, but that's not inevitable. By adopting a few healthy daily habits, they can reverse the damage and live near or at the top of the curve for a good part of their lives.

What Does Wellness Look Like?

Carol Reid worked as a budget specialist in Cleveland Clinic's Operations Department. When she was in her thirties and forties, she found that her weight kept creeping up. By her fiftieth birthday, she weighed 216 pounds—"not morbidly obese, but obese," as she put it. Her husband, Jim, was overweight as well, and it was causing him serious health problems. For 14 years, he had had to make monthly trips to the emergency room to receive treatment for recurring kidney stones. The medication he took to control the pain made it hard for him to function in his daily life. Doctors told him that he'd have fewer stones if he lost weight. On many occasions over the years, he had tried to drop some pounds, but he had not succeeded.

In September 2011, Jim decided to take advantage of a supervised weight-loss regimen offered through Cleveland Clinic's health insurance. The program had him eating high-protein foods, plenty of vegetables, and no sugar. He lost 15 pounds in two weeks. That got Carol's attention. She decided to try it too, and so did the couple's older daughter. Over the course of about nine months, Jim lost 100 pounds, Carol lost 92, and their daughter lost 72. The couple's younger daughter joined in a little later and lost 40 pounds. They had all been carbaholics, but after about a week, Carol said, their craving for carbs settled down. "It's not that hard. Once you find something that works, it becomes easier. It's a life change. You have to think of it as a forever thing."

By 2013, two years after they started, the family members were still maintaining their lower weights. Once they reached their target weights, they were able to reintroduce some foods into their diet. "I feel so much better," Carol reported. "My knees don't hurt. I have more energy. I'm happier, and people tell me that I carry myself differently." She laughed. "I used to need help getting up after bending over to get an item from a low shelf in the grocery store. I don't need that kind of help anymore!" The entire family saw its health improve, including better blood pressure and cholesterol readings. April 2013 marked two years since Jim has had a kidney stone.

Carol had to be at work at 6 every morning. During the workweek, she got up at 3 a.m. and exercised for 45 minutes. She and the rest of her family received ongoing support through Cleveland Clinic's employee wellness program. They saw a nutritionist every two weeks and could e-mail their questions at any time. They had blood testing done, at first every week and then every two weeks. Their insurance covered all this, and, as a result of their success, their premiums decreased. Carol said, "Everyone at the office has been so encouraging, as wellness is a big focus now. It has created a very positive environment for making changes. I didn't jump on the bandwagon right away, but I'm glad I eventually did. It's changed my life!"

When some people hear a word like *wellness*, they tune out. They equate wellness with their mothers telling them to stop watching

TV and eating so much candy. It's about what they *can't* do, they think, pleasures that they *can't* have. But that's wrong. Wellness is a relatively new concept. An older paradigm called "preventive medicine" used to emphasize what not to do—smoke, eat unhealthy foods, or drink too much alcohol.

Wellness is much broader and more positive; it's prevention with an *attitude*—an attitude that embraces life, takes joy in health, and focuses on the pleasures associated with healthy habits. Rather than depriving people of what they enjoy, wellness enriches their lives, teaching them to love their bodies and take pleasure in treating them well. When people are filling every moment of their lives with something healthy that they love doing or eating, there's no room on their plate for that Twinkie or that cheeseburger.

Stubbing Out Tobacco Use

Shortly after I became CEO, Cleveland Clinic decided to take a big first step forward by addressing the problem of smoking. As a young surgeon, I had performed hundreds of lung operations. The normally bright pink, supple tissue of a healthy lung had turned to rigid black in all my patients who smoked—and virtually every one of my patients with lung cancer had done so. My own father had smoked and died of emphysema. I carried the frustration of knowing that it was too late for me to help these patients and my father. So it was personal for me.

In 2004, Cleveland Clinic announced that we were banning smoking in all our hospitals, family health and surgery centers, administrative centers, and parking lots. Employees could not smoke anywhere on the property, not even in their own cars parked on the premises. Security people who encountered smokers on the premises were instructed to ask them not to smoke. Meanwhile, Cleveland Clinic offered free smoking cessation classes and support for any employee who wanted them. In the months leading up to going smoke-free, more than 3,000 employees took advantage of free nicotine replacement patches. Within a year, more than 99 percent of employees and 95 percent of visitors were complying with the policy.

The following year, antismoking advocates in Ohio succeeded in getting an initiative called "Smoke Free Ohio," which sought to ban smoking in all public places, on the state ballot. Support for the initiative was strong, and it appeared to be headed for passage. Then the tobacco industry managed to get another initiative, deceptively named "Smoke Less Ohio," on the ballot. This initiative would have allowed smoking in many public places and would have overturned existing city- and county-level smoking bans. Extensive advertising by the tobacco industry confused people about the content of the two initiatives, making the outcome of the vote uncertain.

Cleveland Clinic's wellness program dispatched physicians to speak on the risks of secondhand smoke, persuaded the local sports teams and the newspaper to endorse the Smoke Free initiative, arranged a news conference on the issue with the previous surgeon general (who had been the author of a report on the risks of secondhand smoke), and engaged an estimated 10,000 employees to do grassroots advocacy through its Employee Wellness Committee network.

This was the first time that Cleveland Clinic had gotten so deeply enmeshed in a burning political issue. Many people didn't like our public stance, and Dr. Roizen reported that he received at least three death threats. Yet in the end, Smoke Free Ohio passed and Smoke Less Ohio was defeated by a "healthy" margin. Newspapers around the state credited Cleveland Clinic for these successes. The people of Ohio had spoken: they wanted wellness.

That favorable outcome emboldened Cleveland Clinic to take the fight even further; we also wanted to do something to reward the residents of the state for their courage. A few weeks later, the institution announced that it would provide free tobacco cessation treatment for residents of Cuyahoga County (which includes Cleveland) for six months starting in January 2007. The state of Ohio would provide free telephone counseling through its "Ohio Quitline," and Cleveland Clinic would provide free nicotine replacement therapy patches to residents who called the Quitline or who were in group programs in county clinics that were not covered by insurance. Cleveland Clinic also provided free access to a web-based tobacco cessation program and donated computers to 22 community centers. Calls to Quitline tripled within the county during the campaign. More than 10,000 smokers participated, 6,600 of whom quit.

In June 2007, following a lengthy period of researching the issues surrounding nonsmoking workplaces, collecting input from employees and managers, and speaking with other companies that had implemented such measures, Cleveland Clinic announced that we would become the first major healthcare provider in the United States to no longer hire smokers.

During a three-month trial period, we tested the nicotine levels of all new hires. Those who tested positive had their job offers rescinded. They were offered free tobacco cessation treatment and encouraged to reapply for employment after they had successfully quit. Since implementing this policy, the organization has had to rescind fewer than 2 percent of all offers. Some smokers have declined to apply for a job at Cleveland Clinic, but 17 times as many people applied for jobs *because* of the policy.

Cuyahoga County used to have one of the highest smoking rates in Ohio, at 26.5 percent. In 2009, it had the lowest rate of any county in the state. Cleveland Clinic's initiatives have saved not only lives but also $330 million a year in area companies' healthcare-related expenses. That meant that area companies had become significantly more competitive compared with firms in states with higher smoking rates.

Within Cleveland Clinic, more than 15 percent of employees used to smoke. In 2013, that number is a little below 6 percent, saving an estimated $7 million in healthcare costs. For every dollar spent on tobacco prevention, the organization realized $4 in savings. Once the smoking rate drops to 2.1 percent, Cleveland Clinic will have saved $36 million in health insurance costs and $114 million by not hiring smokers. The reduction in costs associated with eliminating secondhand smoke is unquantifiable but probably even greater.

Numbers are important, but it's the personal stories of people at Cleveland Clinic and in the wider community who have quit smoking that tell the real story. Karen Whiteley was diagnosed with lung cancer in 2007. She immediately signed up for a smoking cessation class, on her doctor's advice. Her 48-year-old son, David, was with her that day, so he went too. He was a longtime smoker, as was his wife, Sheila. After taking the cessation class with his mother, David found that he really connected with the message. Seeing how awful his mother's cancer was, he decided to quit too, and his wife joined him.

As of 2013, all three of the Whiteleys are *former* smokers. Karen has recovered from her lung cancer and is doing well. David reports feeling much better: "I breathe better, food tastes better, I am able to exercise more, and I don't cough as much anymore." The family has also saved a lot of money; between them, David and Sheila had smoked four to five packs a day, amounting to an outlay of about $25.

David also reports that kicking the habit has given him more self-confidence, which he credited with helping him move up from a job as a laborer to facilities manager. "The counseling is what helped me the most. I learned what triggers me to smoke and how to avoid those triggers. I learned that if I give it a few minutes, the cravings will pass. This has been good for the whole family," David says.

Eating Better, Exercising, and Reducing Stress

From the very beginning, Cleveland Clinic's efforts to eradicate smoking unfolded alongside other wellness efforts. Good nutrition has been a major focus. Upon becoming CEO in 2004, I tried to remove the McDonald's from Cleveland Clinic's lobby. I thought that, as a healthcare provider, we were undeniably sending the wrong message by serving unhealthy fast food to patients and visitors.

As a brand-new, naïve CEO, I didn't realize that we had signed a long-term contract with McDonald's and couldn't just oust them. My attempts to do so sparked controversy in the media, and I became known as the "Big Mac Attacker." I ultimately spoke with McDonald's senior executives, who agreed to some reforms: removing the triple cheeseburger from our McDonald's, changing its advertising, offering salads and apple slices, and eventually using trans-fat-free oil to cook its french fries. It wasn't everything we wanted, but it was good progress.

Of course, a great deal of work remained, which Cleveland Clinic has been accomplishing in phases. Since we were concerned about obesity, we completely revamped our vending machines and cafeterias over a period of several years, eventually making more than 40 changes to our menus and our methods of food preparation. In keeping with Dr. Roizen's prescriptions for healthy eating, the organization phased out sugary foods and those containing trans fats, saturated fats, and nonwhole grains. Removing sugared soda caused sales at the on-site vending machines to drop 60 percent in the first month after these changes. They eventually rose again, stabilizing at a 30 percent decline.

Meanwhile, food items in the cafeteria that met Cleveland Clinic's nutritional guidelines were tagged with a special label: *Go!* inside a green circle. Sales of these food items increased rapidly, leading to use of the label at all Cleveland Clinic sites. It was even employed at a local supermarket chain, where about 1,600 of 33,000 products earned the green *Go!* circle. By 2009, 36 of 55 daily menu items available to patients met the *Go!* criteria, up from zero just a year earlier.

Because fresh foods are the healthiest and most delicious, Cleveland Clinic started a farmers' market at our main campus in 2008, an idea that soon spread to multiple sites. Local unemployed citizens were trained in farming, and two surface lots were converted to "internship in farming sites." In addition, Cleveland Clinic guaranteed all growers farming organically within 115 miles of the main campus that we would purchase all the produce they brought to the farmers' markets that had not been purchased by Cleveland Clinic employees and patients or members of the community.

Exercise is another important focus at Cleveland Clinic. To encourage employees and their dependents to exercise and lose weight, the organization offers free memberships in on-site fitness centers, Curves gyms, and Weight Watchers. On-site fitness center use by cardiac surgeons increased fivefold. The cost of membership hadn't been what prevented these doctors from exercising regularly before—the cultural imperative simply hadn't been there. Now they and the other employees know: Cleveland Clinic values wellness.

The organization has implemented numerous other exercise programs and incentives. We posted signs around many of the elevator banks suggesting that employees take the stairs as a healthier means of transport. Shape Up & Go is a team-based challenge program organized around exercise. All campuses offer free sunrise and sunset yoga classes to anyone who wants to participate. These classes are extremely popular: by mid-2009, almost 70 classes a week were provided to more than 2,000 participants. Additional stress management activities include a "Basics of Personal Economics" class, guided imagery and meditation education and practice, soothing ambient music in all public places, and live concerts several times a week.

Within a year of the launch of many of the exercise programs, employees had lost 144,000 pounds. A year later, they had lost a total of 360,000 pounds. They became fitter, more active, and more vibrant—and happier, too.

Some people have criticized Cleveland Clinic for playing the role of Big Brother with respect to the hard lines we have drawn on smoking, sugary drinks, and other unhealthful items. The critical distinction here is that rather than preventing employees from living their lives as they please, Cleveland Clinic simply refuses to enable unhealthy behavior. Most employees deeply appreciate it.

Employee engagement, a way of measuring how happy employees are at work, has increased. Many employees have commented on how much unanticipated joy they find from living healthier lives. Dr. Roizen reported that he couldn't walk across campus without being approached by grateful employees. Many caregivers at Cleveland Clinic have worked hard to change bad habits and live healthier lives, in the process losing significant amounts of weight and gaining newfound energy. One redcoat greeter stopped smoking after 30 years, thanks to the program. As he reported, "Now I feel better. I look better (I hope). My kids are happy. It's a great feeling."

The Right Incentives

Despite its best efforts, in 2009 Cleveland Clinic was still paying about $400 million in annual healthcare costs, and that figure was increasing at about 6 percent a year. Clearly, this trend was unsustainable. It also came to light that there were 3,000 people with diabetes among Cleveland Clinic's 40,000 employees, and only 15 percent of them were seeing a doctor regularly to manage their condition. As a result, their disease was getting worse, putting a needless burden on the system. Similar trends applied with respect to employees who had other chronic diseases.

To reverse these trends and curb the associated costs, Cleveland Clinic raised the insurance premiums we charge employees by 21 percent, but reduced the premium increases based on how healthy employees were and whether they were enrolled in wellness or disease management programs. Employees who were in good shape and engaged in exercise and other wellness activities saw no premium increase. The premiums of employees with a chronic disease such as diabetes who participated in a wellness program rose only 9 percent. Most notably, employees who had a chronic disease but kept it under control by participating in a free disease management program enjoyed a premium *decrease* of 4 percent.

The savings from these premium changes have been substantial. A chronically ill person could save hundreds of dollars in insurance premiums by taking responsibility for his health. The incentive has worked as hoped—the percentage of employees enrolled in chronic disease management programs has skyrocketed to 60 percent. The incidence of hospitalization among employees with asthma, hypertension, or diabetes has dropped by 20 percent.

Implementing these various wellness incentives has enabled Cleveland Clinic, unlike most other hospitals nationally, to stabilize our healthcare costs. In 2012, our healthcare costs per employee per month remained flat. From 2010 to 2013, our investments in wellness yielded an estimated net $15 million cost savings—a figure that should only increase going forward.

In 2013, Cleveland Clinic rolled out the same incentive program to the spouses of employees, despite anticipated pushback from some employees and their families, who might feel that the organization was meddling too much in their personal lifestyle choices. But Cleveland Clinic knew that this was the right thing to do, both for its employees and for the health of the organization. Employees are more likely to develop and sustain good habits when they are supported by the organization and are surrounded by people who are also taking care of themselves.

Cleveland Clinic is far from the only company that is reaping the rewards of wellness initiatives. Paint manufacturer Sherwin-Williams, another Cleveland organization, unveiled a fitness center at its headquarters, realizing $3 in cost savings and productivity gains for every dollar it spent. Thanks to other wellness initiatives, Sherwin-Williams saw its healthcare costs stabilize, too.[4]

Research has shown that implementing employee wellness plans at large organizations works well in general. Wellness interventions in the United States produce $358 in savings per employee per year but cost employers only $144 per employee per year. Average employee healthcare costs fall by about $3.37 and absenteeism costs fall by about $2.73 for every dollar spent on employee wellness programs. And incentives such as the ones that Cleveland Clinic offers increase participation by employees. From an economic standpoint, wellness is a winning move for any business that is seeking to remain competitive.

The Road Ahead

Cleveland Clinic continues to push both ourselves as an organization and our employees to get healthier. The Wellness Institute is working hard to integrate lifestyle and nutritional counseling into Cleveland Clinic's entire medical practice. The organization has spun off its first wellness businesses as companies, including an e-mail-based coaching company. Extensive informational offerings about wellness are available on the Wellness Institute website.

Finally, Cleveland Clinic's primary care doctors are debuting a wellness widget that spurs patients to answer questions on five wellness topics (smoking, exercise, nutrition, sleep, and depression). The information is entered using a smartphone, a tablet, or the doctor's computer and is integrated with clinical data in the electronic medical record (EMR). Based on patients' responses and information that is already in their EMR, the widget will prompt the doctor to recommend a consultation for a specific wellness issue (for example, smokers would be sent to a tobacco cessation program) or wider care or education options. It also will enable the charting of patients' health to reveal trends over time so that patients and providers can work together to address specific lifestyle and physical concerns.

Cleveland Clinic continues our wellness journey based on our sense that it is our responsibility to our caregivers and patients and to the nation to do so. But wellness is everyone's responsibility. Unfortunately, political leaders could do more. The Affordable Care Act (ACA) has some helpful provisions, such as an annual wellness checkup paid for by Medicare, but essentially the ACA gives medical institutions such as Cleveland Clinic the responsibility for keeping people healthy. Political leaders generally have not been willing to take on the tobacco companies or the food industry as directly as Cleveland Clinic has. Given that roughly 20 percent of the American population still smoke, 60 percent or more are overweight, and the economy is drowning in healthcare costs, America needs much stronger action. As a society, the United States needs to be clear that it's interested in providing *healthcare* for people, not just sick care.

Some tough decisions will need to be made over the next 10 years: either work hard on wellness, or do little, kill the economy, and require sacrifice in vital areas such as education. Choosing wellness seems by far the better route. To make headway, a coalition will be needed, one that includes employers, educators, healthcare providers, legislators, city planners, food processors, and food vendors. Such a coalition can push people to take responsibility for their health and provide the right tools, education, incentives, and leadership.

Ultimately, however, *individuals* must act to take better care of themselves. Those who are already healthy must work to stay that way. Those who need to improve in certain areas should begin their own journey by starting small, taking satisfaction in their victories, and staying the course. Following are some basic action steps that many people can take right away:

1. Those who smoke should talk to their physician about getting into a smoking cessation program.

2. Those who want to exercise more regularly should buy a pedometer and walk 10,000 steps a day. Thirty minutes of weight lifting a week can be added, along with three 20-minute cardio sessions. Enlisting a workout buddy can help support the exercise habit.

3. When visiting their primary care physician, patients should discuss the "five normals": fasting blood sugar, blood pressure, lipids, triglycerides, and body mass index. Anyone who is in the Medicare population should schedule an annual wellness visit.

4. Patients should get 6½ to 8½ hours of sleep a night.

5. Patients should avoid these food ingredients: saturated fats, trans fats, added sugars and syrups, and any grain except 100 percent whole grain.

If the experiences at Cleveland Clinic can show America anything, it's that actions *can* make a difference. All it takes is sustained effort, attention, and determination.

Care Should Take
Place in Different
Settings for Comfort
and Value

One morning in 2013, Ted Carroll (not his real name), a man in his mid-sixties, was awakened from a sound sleep by a sharp, burning pain in his chest that radiated down his left arm. Ted suspected that he was having a heart attack, so he went to the nearest emergency room. At 6:02 a.m., he arrived at the Twinsburg Family Health and Surgery Center in Twinsburg, Ohio, a suburban clinic and outpatient surgery center operated by Cleveland Clinic.

The treatment team moved fast. When someone is having a heart attack, every minute counts. The longer the wait before intervention, the more lasting damage the heart muscle sustains. By 6:06, a nurse had seen and triaged Ted. At 6:10, an emergency room physician gave him an EKG, which confirmed that he was having a heart attack. By 6:18, he had received a chest x-ray. The situation was serious: Ted had a blockage in his left anterior descending artery, which provides the main blood supply to the heart. If doctors couldn't get blood flowing through the artery soon, Ted would die. He needed cardiac catheterization—the placement of a stent into his artery via a catheter inserted in his groin.

Catheterization and the subsequent monitoring and treatment of a heart patient are complex, performed by only 20 percent of the hospitals in the United States; Cleveland Clinic's main campus hospital is one of them. Unfortunately, few hospitals that offer catheterization are able to get a heart attack patient checked in and evaluated, activate a team at the catheterization lab, *and* perform the cardiac procedure, all within an hour. Studies show that approximately a third of all patients don't get the procedure within 90 minutes. Fortunately for Ted, he didn't have to wait that long because, instead of traveling the 25 miles from Twinsburg to Cleveland Clinic's main campus in an ambulance, he could fly there.

Ted had the advantage of being a patient in one of Cleveland Clinic's large regional network of care facilities. At 6:20, a mere 18 minutes after Ted had arrived at Twinsburg, a helicopter containing a fully equipped mobile intensive care unit staffed with intensive care specialists arrived. Working side by side with the Twinsburg Emergency Department staff, the critical care transport team transferred Ted to a cot, started an IV, and gave him aspirin and other vital medications. At 6:30, they took Ted outside and loaded him into the helicopter. By 6:35, the critical care transport team was in the air and flying toward Cleveland at speeds of up to 170 miles an hour. Ten minutes later, Ted and the team arrived at the main campus. He was rushed to a catheterization lab and was handed over to the waiting catheterization team at 6:55. The team members performed the procedure, placing the stent and restoring blood flow to his heart. The catheterization was completed at 7:05—only one hour and three minutes after Ted had arrived at the Twinsburg emergency room.

The Power of a System

Ted owed his life to outstanding caregivers, but to a great extent, he also owed his life to a system. Cleveland Clinic doesn't offer care at only one location; it offers care at a network of facilities spread out across northeastern Ohio (with additional facilities in Florida, Nevada, Toronto, and Abu Dhabi). The system is like a series of concentric circles. In the center is the main campus, which handles the most complex and difficult cases. In the next circle out are the 16 family health centers, where patients can go for routine doctor appointments, noncritical specialty appointments, and some same-day surgeries. Some of them (like Twinsburg) have emergency departments and helipads.

The next circle encompasses Cleveland Clinic's eight community hospitals, which provide hospital and diagnostic services in their respective neighborhoods. These facilities are staffed with both community and Cleveland Clinic doctors. The biggest circle represents patients' homes. As of this writing, the institution is pioneering healthcare that connects Cleveland Clinic with patients at home through electronic monitoring, follow-up visits, and other methods. Its burgeoning array of programs includes a Heart Care at Home program that allows patients like Ted to leave the hospital more quickly following a heart attack. Beyond those programs, Cleveland Clinic's sophisticated online resources provide access to the medical expertise of all Cleveland Clinic caregivers from anywhere in the world.

Cleveland Clinic has been building and refining its network since the 1990s. This has proved fortunate, given that regional healthcare systems are now poised to be the wave of the future. This major shift boils down to economics: the government is increasingly moving to compensate providers based on the *value* that they deliver rather than on the sheer *number* of treatments or procedures that they perform.

The need to provide more value is driving independent hospitals, clinics, and other healthcare providers to join forces. It's a question of survival. Realizing that they can't continue to operate in the same inefficient ways as they have been, they are pooling resources in an attempt to cut costs, improve processes, and make new investments in advanced technology. This consolidation of healthcare has led to the emergence of a few big players, much like what has happened in the electronics, publishing, manufacturing, and food production industries.

Some people believe that bigger is *not* better, but in healthcare, big is good. Small hospitals that aim to serve as "general stores" and offer a little of everything are finding that being "all things to all people" prevents them from getting really good at any one thing. The nation's healthcare system is increasingly rewarding value, not variety at a single site. A large health system can spread its services across multiple sites, concentrating particular services at particular facilities and allowing the caregivers at those facilities to become really good at whatever it is that they do.

By concentrating these more specialized, higher-value providers and closing hospitals that don't add value, integrated health systems can rationalize—and revolutionize—healthcare delivery. Patients receive better-quality, lower-cost care for all their interrelated problems and needs. When they get sick, or as they work to stay well, sophisticated information technology, aircraft, and other infrastructure components that are too expensive for individual hospitals to afford on their own tie the system together as they did for Ted, allowing patients to move seamlessly between locations and medical providers. Cleveland Clinic calls this "the right care, in the right time, at the right place."

Systematic healthcare is also more comfortable care. Less of it takes place in hospitals and more of it occurs at home, in familiar places surrounded by loved ones.

Changing Times, Changing Care

The loss of the local independent hospital is an emotional issue for many people who have deep associations with these institutions. Yet these hospitals are painfully out of date. Most American hospitals were founded at a time when bed rest was considered a cure-all—a view that is in complete contrast to today's wisdom, which says that lying in bed in a building full of sick people is dangerous. It's also increasingly unnecessary because twenty-first-century patients are requiring shorter hospital stays. Many sick patients have chronic diseases that can be managed on an outpatient basis. Medical progress means that even acute episodes such as a heart attack or a broken hip can be treated in ways that require less actual hospitalization, and services such as hospice care can now be provided in a person's home rather than in a care facility.

Specialization is another trend that has turned traditional hospitals into relics of a bygone era. Most community hospitals were opened at a time when treatments were simple and there was only so much that could be done for patients. It was reasonable to expect a hospital to provide appropriate care for all conditions. Over the years, as medicine has branched into numerous disciplines and subdisciplines, the treatments available to patients have multiplied. Technology has advanced and grown more complex. Still, many people expect hospitals to provide every possible service for anyone who walks through the door.

In any industry, the old-fashioned general store model may be a good idea when there's only one merchant in town. But in healthcare, there are thousands of general stores, all competing to offer the full range of services. When everyone offers the same product or service, consumers will often seek out the one with the lowest price, and the various providers will lower their prices accordingly so that they can compete. However, sustaining these lower prices typically requires cutting back in other areas to keep the balance sheet even, which often compromises quality. Consequently, consumers experience a drop in the overall value that they receive. Reduced value in the manufacturing realm might mean that the less expensive product will have to be replaced sooner. In healthcare, the stakes are considerably higher.

One of the most dramatic trends in modern healthcare has been the falling demand for hospital services nationwide. At any given time, hospitals from coast to coast are barely 50 to 60 percent full, yet few hospitals have closed as a result. All patients pay a price for this because it costs a lot of money to pay salaries and keep the lights on at a hospital—costs that are now being spread across too few patients. As one important study found, hospitals capture the largest share of healthcare spending in the United States. They are also responsible for most of the growth in healthcare spending. This study calculated that hospitals account for 41 percent of what Americans overpay for healthcare.

Not only are Americans paying too much for healthcare, they may not be getting the best care possible at a smaller hospital. Hundreds of studies have shown that patients who need complex treatments or risky surgeries do better if they are treated at medical centers that perform more of those treatments or surgeries. This is especially true in the treatment of HIV/AIDS, pancreatic cancer, esophageal cancer, abdominal aortic aneurysms, and congenital heart disease, to name a few conditions. And it makes sense. A center that treats a high volume of patients with these conditions will have more experience, well-organized teams, and well-tested protocols. It will have encountered every potential complication and anatomical variation.

The average community hospital can't develop this kind of experience. It may admit 100 patients a day, but few of those patients will have the same condition. Surgeons in various specialties won't perform enough procedures to stay in good practice and maintain their competence, even if community hospitals are linked with other community hospitals. A group of hospitals might have 150 coronary artery bypass patients a year, but if each hospital in the group has its own cardiac service, those 150 patients will be divided among all the system's hospitals. That means that no single hospital or surgeon will perform more than a handful of some common lifesaving operations.

Competition based on breadth of service is the wrong kind of competition. Patients benefit more from a different kind of competition: value-based competition. A healthcare system provides better value overall by piecing together different kinds of facilities, each of which focuses on performing effectively in its given specialty. Over the entire spectrum of healthcare services, individual patients will receive the best possible care at the lowest cost.

Tabitha's Story

Tabitha McClendon was a woman in her twenties living in Fremont, Ohio. She was born with aortic stenosis, a condition in which the aortic valve in her heart is narrow or does not fully open, decreasing blood flow. As a child living in Iowa, Tabitha saw a doctor on occasion to monitor the condition, but she had never had any symptoms. In 2011, however, after becoming pregnant, she began experiencing shortness of breath, weakness, heart palpitations, and swelling. Her local doctors feared that she might have to have heart surgery while she was still pregnant. They referred her to two Cleveland Clinic physicians: Dr. Amy Merlino, an obstetrician, and Dr. Richard Krasuski, who specializes in adult congenital heart problems.

"Cardiac patients like Tabitha are at increased risk for arrhythmia, heart failure, and even stroke," Dr. Krasuski said. "A number of changes occur during pregnancy—there are dramatic fluid shifts, and the heart has to work exceptionally hard. If necessary, we have medical treatments available—catheter-based treatments and even surgery that can be done during pregnancy." The two doctors monitored Tabitha regularly and determined that she did not require surgery.

Initially, Tabitha received care at one of Cleveland Clinic's suburban outpatient family health clinics, Chestnut Commons, and then at Fairview, a community hospital in the network. As Dr. Merlino explained, "We were able to do the ultrasounds at Chestnut Commons to follow the baby's growth and continually monitor the risk of low birth weight. Tabitha went to Fairview Hospital so that the pediatricians there could do an echocardiogram of the baby to check for heart problems." They found none, but as her pregnancy progressed, Tabitha continued to experience shortness of breath and other symptoms.

The doctors and Tabitha were afraid that a normal vaginal birth or even a cesarean done under local anesthesia would put too much strain on her heart. They decided that she should deliver her baby by cesarean section under general anesthesia. They would perform the operation at the unique Special Delivery Unit at Cleveland Clinic Children's on the main campus.

Created in 2012, the Special Delivery Unit exemplifies Cleveland Clinic collaboration. It is the first unit of its kind in Ohio and one of only a few in the nation that bring together a multidisciplinary team of maternal-fetal medicine specialists, fetal radiologists, neonatologists, geneticists, pediatric surgeons, and advanced practice nurses to manage complex maternal-fetal cases from initial consultation through delivery and recovery. Other specialists, such as cardiologists or oncologists, are brought in as needed.

"A lot of units specialize in caring for high-risk newborns," Dr. Merlino explained. "What makes this unit so innovative is that we can provide care for both critically ill newborns and critically or potentially sick moms. So if you have a baby diagnosed with a birth defect who needs to go to surgery immediately after delivery or a mom who may require specialized care herself, we can provide that for them at our main campus. We even have the ability to perform both emergency open-heart surgery on the newborn and emergency open-heart surgery on the mother—at the same time. We work with a team of specialists for the specific complex care that's needed. We can provide mothers with the most normal birthing experience they can have, given their complex situation, and we are able to attend to mom and baby in the same facility for the remainder of their care."

In Tabitha's case, all went well. She gave birth to a healthy seven-pound, eight-ounce girl whom she named Olivia Rose. Doctors were concerned that the baby might have aortic stenosis as well, but another echocardiogram showed that her heart was normal. Olivia was taken to the neonatal intensive care unit (even though she was healthy), and Tabitha went to the cardiac intensive care unit for 24 hours of monitoring. She was moved to a more typical room after that and was finally able to spend some time with her baby. In October 2012, Tabitha underwent heart surgery to replace her faulty valve. She came out of the surgery in great shape, and as of 2013, both mother and daughter are healthy.

The care that Tabitha received was both better and more cost-effective than what she would have gotten 10 years earlier at Cleveland Clinic. During the 1990s, babies were delivered at six hospitals in the network, including the main campus. Based on statistics showing that some community hospitals had only about 20 births a month while others had 80 or more, Cleveland Clinic realized that these hospitals were operating inefficiently. The hospitals with 20 births had a higher rate of complications because obstetrics personnel had less experience in delivering babies. They weren't working optimally as a team, since they had not had the opportunity to establish routines and protocols that would enable them to act instinctively.

In looking at all its hospitals as a system, Cleveland Clinic decided to consolidate routine, low-risk births at two locations. Not surprisingly, complication rates decreased. Also, every step of the process improved, from making an appointment to receiving care and discharge instructions. At these two locations, staff members didn't see delivering babies as an interruption of their day; it was all they did, every day. Because they saw a predictable number of low-risk pregnancies, they could develop predictable processes and purchase predictable amounts of supplies, which in turn lowered costs.

Using the same systems approach, Cleveland Clinic also enhanced its performance with respect to high-risk pregnancies such as Tabitha's. Moving routine obstetrics off the main campus freed up space there to construct more sophisticated delivery rooms for complicated births and to expand the neonatal intensive care unit for frail and premature babies. As a result, obstetrics personnel on the main campus were gaining much more experience with difficult births. Whereas before staff members might have seen one or two difficult births a year, now they were seeing one or two a week. This increase in experience led to fewer complications, lower costs, and better outcomes.

Cleveland Clinic patients now have the best of both worlds. They can go to a community hospital for excellent routine care, an option that lets them stay closer to home. If their pregnancy becomes high risk, they can go to the main campus for leading-edge care that is now even better than before—all while the system as a whole operates more efficiently, at a lower overall cost.

As it consolidated deliveries in fewer locations, Cleveland Clinic also took steps to standardize and improve the care that it provided. It brought together obstetrics leaders to work on reducing the number of cesarean births. Cesarean births result in more complications than vaginal births do, and they cost about 70 percent more on average. In 2010, it standardized the reporting of data on births, then developed a checklist, which was implemented in 2011, to screen women for cesareans more effectively in order to reduce the number of women who had the procedure on an elective basis. Within a year, the organization reached its goal of reducing the number of elective cesarean births to less than 5 percent of all births.

Obstetrics is only one example of how Cleveland Clinic is using a systemic approach to improve care. It has consolidated much of its neurology and neurosurgery services at the main campus and at two hubs, which are strategically located on opposite sides of the metro area. As of 2013, patients who have a stroke in the Cleveland area can receive high-quality standard stroke care at any of Cleveland Clinic's hospitals, all of which are Certified Stroke Centers. Patients whose stroke requires more specialized care will be transferred to one of the neurology hubs, where they will have the same seamless experience that Ted Carroll had during his heart attack.

Toward Better Integration

In the early stages of building its healthcare system, Cleveland Clinic consolidated a number of area community hospitals under the Cleveland Clinic name, but in many respects these units were still operating as independent entities. The fact that the organization was using two logos was a symbol of the disjointedness of the consolidation. The organization ultimately combined elements of both logos to create the current design. It was a seemingly small change, but it represented the larger work that lay ahead to combine Cleveland Clinic's many assets and resources into "One Cleveland Clinic."

Four ingredients were essential to integrating these various entities: information technology (the electronic medical record), critical care transport, care paths, and the patient-centered medical home.

Cleveland Clinic invested a substantial amount of money in its highly developed electronic medical record. That investment has enabled caregivers to keep track of patients anywhere in the system, from the moment they arrive to the moment they are discharged and beyond. Suppose, for example, that an older man who has been in a car accident arrives on the main campus for treatment. During the course of that treatment, care providers learn that the patient has diabetes and lives 30 miles away. After discharging him from the main campus hospital, they can continue to monitor both his injuries and his diabetes at the rehabilitation clinic because the doctors there have the same information about the patient as the emergency room doctors did. Later, when the patient seeks outpatient care for his diabetes, his doctor would continue to be informed about every point of contact the patient has with Cleveland Clinic's healthcare system.

"A SYSTEM OPEN TO ANYONE"

The electronic medical record enables Cleveland Clinic to extend healthcare access to patients who live anywhere in the world. William Einziger, a principal engineer at General Electric, was in a car accident while traveling with his wife and one of his daughters. All three were transported by ambulance to the nearest hospital. There, William and his family underwent a series of tests that ultimately showed that none of them had been seriously injured in the crash. William, however, received deeply troubling news. The CT scan he underwent during his emergency room visit had revealed a mass on his right kidney. He had had no symptoms and no pain, and he certainly wasn't aware that something was growing inside him.

William was immediately referred to a urological oncologist near his hometown in South Carolina. At his first appointment days later, the surgeon told William that there was a 90 percent chance that the tumor was malignant and that he felt most comfortable removing the entire right kidney, a procedure that is also known as a radical nephrectomy. The surgeon predicted that with this procedure, there was a 95 percent chance that the cancer would not recur. "I felt confused and overwhelmed by the surgeon's recommendations,"

William said. "Only days before that, I had had no idea that I had cancer. Now, I was faced with the choice of losing a whole kidney." He wasn't sure what this meant for his future.

William reached out to a family friend who was also a urologist to voice his concerns. His physician friend suggested that William research a procedure known as a partial nephrectomy, which would remove only a portion of the kidney. Shortly after speaking with his friend, William remembered hearing about a benefit that was covered under the healthcare plan offered to him by his employer that would allow him to receive a second opinion on his renal mass and recommendations for the most appropriate treatment.

That covered benefit was the MyConsult Online Medical Second Opinion program. This secure online program provides medical second opinions from Cleveland Clinic specialists for more than 1,200 diagnoses that may affect quality of life or that may be more serious.

"I have to admit that I was skeptical about trying the MyConsult program because I was told it would take too much time to receive my second opinion," William said. "I had a new cancer diagnosis. I didn't have time to spare, and I wanted treatment as soon as possible." A General Electric health coach assured William that his case would be triaged immediately by the registered nurses on the MyConsult Clinical Operations team and that he would receive his electronic second opinion report from a Cleveland Clinic specialist securely and as quickly as possible.

Within a few days of sending his health records and test results to the MyConsult team, William received some exciting news from Dr. Robert Stein, codirector of robotic surgery in the Department of Urology at Cleveland Clinic's Glickman Urological & Kidney Institute. Dr. Stein believed that he could save the majority of William's right kidney by removing only the tumor and leaving the normal kidney tissue alone. The robotic procedure would be minimally invasive, requiring only a few small incisions, as opposed to the large incision required for the radical nephrectomy.

"I was still confused over which procedure I should have, so I read several research reports on the Internet, as well as the references on the Cleveland Clinic website concerning radical versus partial nephrectomy. They all indicated that partial nephrectomy was an effective treatment for kidney cancer," William said. "Dr. Stein told me that I would still have 70 percent of my right kidney following the surgery. To me, having 1.7 kidneys seemed more promising than having only one."

After confirming that his local urologist would be able to provide the appropriate follow-up care, William called Cleveland Clinic to schedule his minimally invasive robotic partial nephrectomy for two weeks later. His local urologist and Dr. Stein conferred on the phone. After surgery, William spent a few days in the hospital recovering. When he returned home to South Carolina, he felt weak and fatigued, but he was extremely happy that the majority of his right kidney had been spared and that he probably would not need chemotherapy or radiation. He gained strength as he continued his recovery, walking laps around his house and going up and down the stairs. Soon he was walking up to three miles a day with his wife. Five weeks after surgery, William returned to work on a part-time basis, and he started full time after eight weeks.

Electronic medical records are important, but integration can't exist solely in cyberspace. Cleveland Clinic's critical care transport—like the helicopter that zipped Ted Carroll from the suburbs to the main campus during his heart attack—physically links the various entities throughout the organizational network and is the second ingredient required for successful integration. The fleet includes ambulances that can transport patients to and between facilities and jets that can bring them to Ohio from anywhere in the world. The motto is, "No patient too sick, no patient too far." As of 2013, the planes had picked up patients in more than 40 states and 20 countries. The medical teams onboard the jets can transport patients on ventilators, perform lab tests, put in temporary pacemakers, and run diagnostic imaging—all while flying tens of thousands of feet above the earth.

A third ingredient in the integration of Cleveland Clinic's various entities has been the development and implementation of care paths to standardize procedures for delivering care. Care paths ensure that patients will receive the same standard of care for their ailment or condition regardless of which Cleveland Clinic facility they enter. Care paths ensure that all caregivers are on the same page and that the patient is treated in ways that have been shown to provide the best outcome at the lowest cost. The development of care paths is ongoing, with the goal being that care paths will eventually be available for dozens, if not hundreds, of medical areas, dramatically enhancing the value that Cleveland Clinic can offer and ensuring high quality no matter where in the network patients seek care.

Affirming the importance of care paths doesn't mean that institutions should provide all patients with exactly the same treatment, regardless of an individual's specific condition, or that individual doctors should adhere at all times to a single protocol handed down from on high. Obviously, every patient is different, and in some dimensions of care, doctors need to make intuitive judgments about what a specific patient requires. But standardizing care makes sense for many conditions, like strokes, where it yields better quality and reduced cost across the entire system.

Dr. Michael Modic, chair of the Neurological Institute, offered this analogy: "I think of a care path as being like one big highway.

There may be different off-ramps and different lanes. One size doesn't fit all. But having a common highway that everyone at Cleveland Clinic can drive on offers big advantages in reducing unnecessary variations in the care that people receive—variations that decrease the overall value of this care."

A final ingredient in integrating Cleveland Clinic's various locations into one well-functioning system is the patient-centered medical home. This concept, which is not unique to Cleveland Clinic, is a model of primary care that assigns each patient a team that stays with her throughout her care, no matter where in the system the patient may go.

Patients who use Cleveland Clinic for primary care are monitored by a team that might include a primary care or specialty physician, nurse-practitioners, physician assistants, medical assistants, registered nurses, care coordinators, and pharmacists. The care coordinator has a key role in making sure that other staff members understand the patient's preferences for care, that clinical goals are set, and that the right interventions are implemented. In recognition of how complicated medications can be, the team includes a pharmacist to help patients manage chronic conditions such as high blood pressure, diabetes, and congestive heart failure.

In the patient-centered medical home model, a primary care physician is notified when his patient is admitted to the hospital. Even if another doctor cares for the patient in the hospital, the primary care physician still provides the patient's follow-up care. When a patient goes to a rehab or skilled nursing facility, the whole team is there along the way to ensure that the care given is consistent and appropriate. If a patient needs to see a certain specialist on an outpatient basis, the team makes sure that the patient gets there.

Team members establish deep relationships with patients over time, helping them prevent disease by talking to them about their lab work, diet, exercise, and medication. And because an entire team is at work, physicians have more personal time to spend with patients. At all times, patients have direct access to caregivers who know their problems and their medical history and who really care about them as individuals. Patient-centered medical homes are all about helping patients use the many resources at their disposal to become and stay healthy.

More Time at Home

Patient-centered medical homes work. Patients regularly report how much they love this concept. Perhaps the single biggest reason that people feel comfortable in a health system like Cleveland Clinic's is that it allows them to spend more time in their *own* homes and less time in a hospital. Despite the most valiant attempts to make a hospital a pleasant, healing space, it can never be as comfortable, familiar, or reassuring as one's own home.

With the availability of advanced technologies and techniques and an integrated system that includes a wide range of resources, including outpatient centers, doctors' offices, local pharmacies, and visiting nurse and doctor services, patients don't need to spend as much time in the hospital as they have in the past. Many conditions can be managed expertly by doctors and other medical professionals on an outpatient basis. In fact, medical research reports that when a skilled team of specialists provides home healthcare, patients recover more quickly, experience better outcomes, and are more satisfied with the experience. What follows is one patient's story.

John Cromer, a 71-year-old retired engineer from Canton, Ohio, was becoming a "couch potato" as a result of severe knee pain. His doctors decided that he needed to have a separate surgery to replace each of his knees. Normally, patients who undergo this surgery have to spend up to three weeks in a rehabilitation facility—at a cost that equals or exceeds the cost of the surgery. This long time away from home can be discouraging, sometimes leading to physical inactivity and depression.

Because of a new "rapid recovery" program that was in place at one of Cleveland Clinic's community hospitals, John had to remain in the hospital for only three days after each surgery. Upon his release, instead of traveling back to the hospital three days a week for rehabilitation, he was able to complete in-home physical therapy for three weeks. Cleveland Clinic arranged for a physical therapist to come to his house on a schedule that suited him. This allowed John to spend time with his wife of 47 years as well as his two children and one grandchild.

As John remembered, "I just figured, why stay in the hospital after surgery longer than I needed to? I was spending my time [in the hospital] eating, taking my medication, bathing, and doing physical therapy. I could do all that at home. Being able to do physical therapy at home helped my healing a lot—it was a big psychological boost. Plus, my doctor told me I'd face a higher risk of infection in the hospital than I would at home. So why not? As long as you have someone at home to help you, you can do it. The physical therapist mapped out everything I needed to focus on in order to recover. It was beyond my expectations."

After the initial rehabilitation period, John undertook more traditional physical therapy at an outpatient facility near his home—nine weeks for one knee and six weeks for the other. Traveling more than an hour to the main campus for his surgeries was worth the trip for John, as he had researched his Cleveland Clinic doctor and trusted his skills. But making that trip repeatedly during his many weeks of physical therapy would have been far more of a burden on him.

As John's surgeon, Dr. Mark Froimson, related, Cleveland Clinic's rapid recovery program for hip and knee replacement doesn't push patients out of the hospital whether or not they are ready to go. Instead, staff members create a discharge plan for managing the patients after surgery, prepare patients and their families to follow the plan, and make the necessary arrangements in advance of the patients' discharge.

"Our job is to return patients to their homes as soon as it's safe. It turns out that if you educate them properly and make appropriate resources available to them, most patients can safely return home from the hospital after two or three days. The old notion of having to go to a rehab hospital after surgery as the default is actually wrong. We're moving to a system in which you come to the hospital for this surgery, we educate you about safety and pain management, we organize your rehab, we send someone to your house to check for safety, we get your family to support you, and we allow you to go home within a few days, or as soon as it's safe. It's about empowering the patient to succeed rather than just putting her in a rehab facility."

As of 2013, the program is working. The number of patients who go directly home has increased, improving patient satisfaction while decreasing readmissions to the hospital. Quality of care is up, and cost of treatment is down. As for John, he has become much more active than he was before his surgeries. He is "restarting his retirement," as he put it, playing golf again and taking vacations. Home care—and staying out of the hospital—worked well for him.

Cleveland Clinic provides opportunities for home-based care for many conditions and illnesses. The Center for Connected Care focuses on keeping patients connected to the highest-quality care as they make the transition from the hospital to home or to a post-acute care facility. The center, which in 2013 includes more than 400 caregivers who provide daily care to 12,000 patients, consolidates a number of home and transitional care services.

Its Hospice at Home service provides end-of-life care to patients in their homes instead of in a traditional institutional setting. Medical Care at Home has revived the traditional house call for patients who are too sick or too frail to get to a doctor's office. Previously, a patient who required intravenous medication had to go to a hospital or a clinic, but the Infusion Pharmacy at Home program has changed that. Patients who need advanced respiratory therapy, wound care, or diabetes support can receive those services at home, too.

The Heart Care at Home program is one of the center's most innovative. Founded in 2010, the program allows heart failure patients to make the transition from the hospital to their everyday lives more effectively. While patients are still hospitalized, a nurse affiliated with the program meets with them about medication and other issues involved in going home. Within a few days of discharge, a member of the team arrives at the patient's home and installs equipment that measures the patient's weight, blood pressure, heart rate, and other vital signs. This information is relayed to a central website that is monitored by healthcare providers. During the first month after discharge, team members call the patient to check in on a regular basis—more frequently if something is going wrong.

Although Cleveland Clinic is continuing to collect data on how well heart patients have fared when they are monitored at home, preliminary results indicate that patients who are continuously monitored through a program like Heart Care at Home experience fewer readmissions and better outcomes. They also spend fewer days in the hospital. They enjoy the peace of mind that comes with knowing that their caregivers are keeping tabs on their condition and are never far away. "Heart Care at Home gave me back my life," one patient said. "I felt like I had lost control of my health, and Heart Care at Home gave me back that control. I had people to call when I needed help, and I was able to stay at home. I received counseling and teaching by phone that helped me make better choices. I have a new lease on life!"

Big Medicine Is Better Medicine

Medicine is personal, but it's also a business, and it would do well to apply relevant and proven methods from other industries. Companies such as FedEx, Whole Foods, and Apple are examples of large, innovative organizations that have changed consumers' lives for the better. They compete to supply services across a broad geographic area; they leverage economies of scale in cost, distribution, and supply; and they innovate constantly and disseminate new policies and procedures quickly across all of their locations. Each of these brands is a byword for quality, efficiency, and reliability. As a result, each satisfies the needs of more customers more efficiently than smaller enterprises can.

Caring for millions of patients involves numerous complexities that make medicine a very different business from, say, software development, but both can benefit from applying the principles described. For medicine, that means integrating healthcare providers into large regional systems to organize the available resources more efficiently and sensibly, bringing together medical centers, community hospitals, local clinics, doctors' offices, pharmacies, and other providers in such a way as to enable them to do what they do best in a coordinated way.

Healthcare systems can greatly improve the care that they provide while eliminating needless waste. And they can do so while offering patients the technology, knowledge, and other resources that they need if they are to stay out of hospitals and stay healthier on their own.

The organizational theorist and business thinker Peter Senge wrote, "Business and human endeavors are also systems . . . we tend to focus on snapshots of isolated parts of the system, and wonder why our deepest problems never seem to get solved."[1] It's time for America to focus much less on maintaining the traditional freestanding hospital and much more on creating networks of care providers. Also, the focus should increasingly shift to the elements that tie these networks together and enable them to function as *more* than the sum of their parts.

The relationship of doctor and patient will always be sacred, and there is no substitute for the healing touch of a truly compassionate caregiver. But medicine is moving away from the severely localized model of care. A medical center is no longer a single brick-and-mortar building; it is now a system that is spread across space and time. Cleveland Clinic physicians on earth have even performed electrocardiography on astronauts in the International Space Station.

All academic medical centers, hospital systems, hospitals, and group practices in the United States must begin to discuss how to coordinate their activities and resources on a larger scale to lower their costs and provide better patient care. America's patients and everyday citizens can participate through an awareness and appreciation of how regional integrated systems can improve the health of whole populations. As President John F. Kennedy once said, "What unites us is far greater than what divides us."[2] People and organizations accomplish so much more when they put aside competition and work together.

Care Should Be
Tailor-Made for You

n May 2013, actress Angelina Jolie announced some startling news. In an op-ed published in the *New York Times* titled "My Medical Choice," she told the world that she had recently had surgery to remove both of her breasts. The procedure is called a double mastectomy. Thousands of women who have been diagnosed with invasive breast cancer have it done every year, usually followed by surgeries to reconstruct their breasts. But Angelina did not have cancer. She was perfectly healthy. She had taken this drastic step because she had undergone genetic testing and been found to have mutations in a gene called *BRCA1*.

In the vast majority of female patients, breast cancer is probably caused by multiple factors. Possible risk factors include having denser breast tissue, being exposed to certain toxins, using birth control pills, and being overweight. But in up to 5 to 10 percent of patients, genetics plays a strong role. Women who inherit mutations in certain genes, most notably *BRCA1*, have a dramatically increased risk of contracting breast and ovarian cancer at an early age and dying from it. Angelina's mother had passed away from cancer at age 56, having been diagnosed when she was in her forties. As Angelina revealed, her doctors had presented her with a cold, hard truth: she had an 87 percent chance of developing breast cancer and a 50 percent chance of developing ovarian cancer.

Angelina didn't have to have her breasts removed. It was a preventive choice that she made. Other options that women in her position can consider include receiving preventive chemotherapy and holistic treatments. Angelina chose surgery because she decided that it would "minimize the risk" as much as possible. According to her doctors, the procedures reduced her chance of contracting breast cancer to below 5 percent. "I can now tell my children that they don't need to fear they will lose me to breast cancer," Angelina remarked.[1]

Many of us at Cleveland Clinic took notice of Angelina's announcement—and not just because we count ourselves as fans of her work. Her experience directed public attention to an area that we believe represents the exciting frontier of twenty-first-century medicine. It's called personalized (or precision) healthcare. Traditionally, most doctors have taken a "one size fits all" approach to treating patients. When you get sick, for instance, you're usually given medications that have been evaluated on the basis of how well they work in a large population of people. When you go in for your annual physical, you're given advice on how to prevent chronic diseases that is based on what we know holds true for patients in general. But people aren't all the same. We're similar in some ways and different in others. We each have personal preferences about how we want to be treated, and we each have basic genetic differences that affect how likely our bodies are to get sick and how well they will respond to certain medications. Each of us, like Angelina Jolie, has genetic abnormalities that predispose us to certain illnesses and lower our risks of contracting others. Personalized healthcare is a movement to offer care that is adapted much more closely to the wonderfully complex nuances of patients' bodies and needs.

The technology that is driving personalized healthcare is only in its infancy, but it's developing fast. In 2003, the Human Genome Project succeeded in mapping a complete set of human DNA, including all its genes—called a genome—at a cost of $4 billion. In 2009, sequencing a human genome was projected to cost only about $100,000. By 2012, that figure was $10,000 or less.[2] By 2020, the price is likely to drop below $1,000—to about the cost of a routine MRI. Already, you can have parts of your genome sequenced for under $100.[3] Advances in big data and big analytics mean that we're also getting better at figuring out which genetic defects or combinations of genetic markers correlate with which specific diseases. Meanwhile, the widespread use and refinement of the electronic medical record as a clinical tool means that we're increasingly able to apply genetic information to caring for patients in real time.

In the years ahead, we're going to learn much more about the genetic makeup of individual patients. We're going to use that information to provide higher-quality and less costly care. We'll have many more tests such as the one Angelina Jolie had, and they will cost less (Angelina's test cost about $3,000 and looked at only 2 of the 35,000 human genes). Our understanding of the genetic basis for disease will completely transform the treatment and prevention of many diseases.

Yet personalized healthcare is not only about advanced genomics. It involves many things that Cleveland Clinic and other leading medical organizations are already doing and will be doing to put the focus of care on the individual patient. Dr. Kathryn Teng, director of the Center for Personalized Healthcare at Cleveland Clinic, explains that personalized healthcare includes "the effort to learn and record a patient's genetic information, personal and family medical history, health-related behaviors, culture, and values—and to use that information as an individual risk prediction tool for the more precise management of disease care."[4]

Think about the systemic approach to medicine described in the previous chapter, which aims to provide the right care, at the right time, in the right place. With personalized healthcare, we're going to get much better at providing the first two pieces: the right care at the right time. Just as the resources of large medical systems will allow these organizations to provide more comfortable and familiar care, they will also enable them to know more about each patient and give each one exactly what he needs if he is to stay healthy. This, in turn, will help lower costs. In the exciting future of healthcare, we won't be treated like numbers. We'll be treated like the unique human beings that we are.

How Personalized Care Works

Physicians have long taken family history and habits into account in making their diagnoses and in offering tailored advice on how to prevent disease.[5] Personalized healthcare will enable medical professionals to increase the value that patients receive for their healthcare dollars.

Dr. Charis Eng is a distinguished geneticist who has discovered several of the genes that when mutated lead to cancer. She is also the founding chair of Cleveland Clinic's Genomic Medicine Institute and director of its clinical arm, the Center for Personalized Genetic Healthcare, which performs patient-oriented scientific research and translates that into clinical care. As Dr. Eng notes, ancient Chinese healers understood the importance of looking for personal information that might indicate how specific individuals would respond to specific treatments. As is written in the *Huang Ti Nai Ching*, the first recorded Chinese medical text, dating from 2,600 BC: "Superior doctors prevent the disease. Mediocre doctors treat the disease before evident. Inferior doctors treat the full blown disease."[6] Modern technology makes it possible to understand human disease in much greater depth than ancient healers could.

Personalized healthcare has been in the making since the mid-twentieth century, when Francis Crick and James Watson first drew the double helix. By 2011, scientists had identified some 3,000 genes that predisposed people to certain illnesses *on a molecular level.* Using this knowledge, we can now predict who is at risk and either prevent people from getting sick or diagnose the condition early, when it is treatable.[7] We have made particular strides in predicting cancer risk by taking a genomic approach. In the future, we'll apply this same approach to other conditions.

We used to think of diseases as being either "common" or "rare." Thanks to our emerging genomic understanding of the body, we are starting to see all disease as a collection of subsets of relatively rare disorders that we can potentially treat and prevent in more tailored ways. This approach can make treatment much more effective. When doctors treat all patients suffering from a particular illness in the same basic way, if standard treatments don't work, the doctors have to do their best to adapt them or try new treatments. It becomes a process of trial and error, leading in too many cases to poor outcomes and money wasted on ineffective treatments. As Dr. Teng reflects, "We're going to move from a trial-and-error approach to more of a targeted, precise strategy. What we need to do from here is take our discoveries about the genome, develop new treatment approaches, and help doctors incorporate those approaches into their practices."

We're already seeing this happen. Fifty years ago, doctors thought of breast cancer as a single disease that worked the same way in all patients. Now we know that some people have tumors with different genetic markers that make them more receptive to certain therapies than to others. So now we put breast cancer patients into different categories and give them customized therapies. Likewise, we know that some forms of melanoma—a deadly form of skin cancer—are genetically programmed to be resistant to treatment, whereas others respond very well to treatment. Accordingly, the prognoses we can make and the treatments we can provide will differ for different patients. We understand that a certain genetic defect causes people to have Lynch syndrome. This condition predisposes people to developing colorectal, uterine, stomach, and ovarian cancers. Through genetic testing, we can determine whether a patient has Lynch syndrome and then take preventive steps to avoid cancer and save a life.[8]

Assessing Risk and Preventing Disease

Personalized healthcare can be divided into three distinct clinical applications: the assessment of risk based on personal and family health histories, the customization of therapies, and getting patients more involved in and engaged with their own care.

The first application is the assessment of risk based on personal and family health histories. This allows doctors to decide whether to go forward with genetic testing, similar to what Angelina Jolie had done, and to determine which test to perform. So far, we have a limited capability in this area. Approximately 10 percent of diseases are true hereditary genetic diseases—illnesses in which we can identify the cause as one or more specific and strong genes. Most diseases, however, are what scientists call "multifactorial"— they are caused by many factors, although genes may play a part. Scientists such as Dr. Eng are identifying more and more genes that cause disease, increasing our ability to determine an individual's risk and take preventive steps. We're also making much more systematic use of family history, which studies have shown can help us determine disease risk quite well.

One area in which doctors are making progress in assessing risk is asthma. As of 2013, researchers had found links between 15 specific genes and asthma. They found that people who had these genes had a significantly higher risk of suffering from chronic asthma as adults. Researchers emphasized that they were still far from developing a test that could be useful in a clinical setting. In particular, they expected that more genes that increased the risk of asthma would be discovered. Down the road, though, it's possible to imagine that we might one day test our children early on to know whether their breathing problems are likely to persist throughout adulthood. That, in turn, would aid in treatment.[9]

To understand why genetic testing holds so much potential, let's consider a situation for which a reliable test already exists. Stew Mellick (not his real name) is a 40-year-old man who came to Cleveland Clinic for a preventive care visit. He was healthy and felt well, but he was concerned because his older brother had died un-expectedly of a heart attack at age 45. His brother had had no medi-cal conditions that Stew was aware of, although he remembered that his brother looked "tan" in his last year despite living in Vermont. As part of Stew's wellness visit, his primary care physician explored his family history in more depth. Stew had only one sibling (the one who had recently died). His mother had died of liver failure at age 50, although she was not known to be a heavy drinker. His father was still alive. His mother's parents were both deceased: his mater-nal grandfather had died of a heart attack early (just before age 45), and his maternal grandmother had died of a stroke when she was in her seventies. Stew had one child, a daughter, age 20.

Based on this family history, Stew's primary care physician sus-pected a common genetic condition called hemochromatosis, a disorder in which iron builds up to abnormally high levels in the arteries and organs. This can lead to cirrhosis of the liver and early heart attacks. He checked Stew's iron levels and found them to in fact be high. The physician then referred Stew to a medical genet-icist, who confirmed the family history, counseled Stew about the implications of genetic testing, and had a genetic test run to con-firm the diagnosis. Stew's genetic test returned positive for the hemochromatosis gene mutations. Based on all these results, his physician sent him for a treatment to reduce his iron stores and prevent organ damage. Also based on his results, his daughter was advised to have regular blood tests to monitor her iron levels.

Stew's case is a classic example of using genomics to ad-dress a specific familial condition. But what about that even more widespread and widely feared collection of diseases—cancer? Dr. Brian Bolwell is chair of Cleveland Clinic's Taussig Cancer Institute. As he told me, "The new cancer treatments we're already seeing thanks to genomics are exciting. But I believe the biggest potential of genomics is in helping us prevent illness. Most cancers take a long time to develop—10 to 15 years or more. If we can figure out genomic abnormalities that occur during that latency period and detect them, we can potentially prevent disease from ever occurring. Cancer is generally tricky to treat. The best treatment is always prevention or very early treatment, before the cancer has spread. There is the real possibility that we'll see some big wins in the area of cancer prevention going forward."

People are sometimes leery of genetic testing. They fear that insurance companies and employers might learn about their genetic status and discriminate against them on that basis. However, since 2008 we've had a U.S. law, the Genetic Information Nondiscrimination Act, that prevents discrimination in employment and health insurance based on genetic information. Many people also don't like the idea of genetic testing because they fear they will find out that they have an elevated risk of developing a devastating illness. But suppose you had a gene that significantly increases your risk for a heart attack—wouldn't you want to start on a diet that would be appropriate for avoiding coronary artery disease? Even if you had a gene for Alzheimer's, for which there is currently no cure, wouldn't you want to at least know about it so that you could plan for it and make appropriate choices? I know I would—which is why I had myself tested to learn about my disease risk.

In the years ahead, we're going to understand more and more about the physiological hands that we as individuals have been dealt. The challenge will be to collect as much data about people as possible so that we can observe relationships between disease processes and genetic makeup, and do so in a way that protects people's privacy.

Personalizing Treatment—Matt's Story

The second application of personalized healthcare is the customization of therapies. Breast cancer is one example, but there are others. The new field of pharmacogenetics is devoted to discovering genetically based differences in how people metabolize different drugs. This will help us understand which medicines will work for which people, which people will experience which side effects, and how severe those side effects will be. We at Cleveland Clinic have been fortunate enough to see an incredible early example of the promise of customized therapies.

In 2011, 25-year-old Matt Hiznay, a medical student in Ohio, came down with a cough that he couldn't shake. After cough drops didn't help, he went to the doctor and was given news that none of us want to hear: he had cancer. He then went to Cleveland Clinic to receive care from Dr. Nathan Pennell, a thoracic oncologist. The news was even worse. He had stage IV lung cancer. The disease was rapidly spreading throughout his body. He already had it in both lungs, in his lymph nodes, and in his breastbone.

Over the next three weeks, Matt dropped 30 pounds and was admitted to intensive care. He was dying—too weak even for conventional chemotherapy. As Matt has written, "Dr. Pennell later told me that I experienced all the complications a lung cancer patient experiences—but whereas they usually occur over several years, mine all occurred in a matter of five days."[10]

When Dr. Pennell first saw Matt, he did something that cancer doctors never used to do: he tested for a specific genetic mutation that scientists were then just beginning to implicate in lung cancer. The *ALK* gene causes tumor cells to thrive and spread. Most lung cancer is caused by years of smoking, but Matt was a nonsmoker and was very young to be contracting lung cancer. A hereditary genetic defect might well have been the culprit.

Two weeks later, the test results revealed that Matt did in fact carry this mutation. Fortunately for him, the government had just approved a new cancer drug specifically for patients with the *ALK* mutation. As Matt has explained, "This miracle drug, called crizotinib, blocks the mutated *ALK* gene in my cancer cells. Crizotinib is not your typical chemotherapy. Whereas traditional intravenous chemotherapy attacks all fast-dividing cells, whether the cells are cancerous or not, crizotinib attacks only the cancerous cells in my body. Crizotinib saved my life."

Dr. Pennell didn't have to try different chemotherapy drugs to find the one that would work best in Matt. He could prescribe a drug that was tailored specifically to Matt's genetic problem.

Within two weeks of starting crizotinib, Matt had recovered enough to leave the hospital. Two months later, he had no sign of cancer. In May 2012, his cancer came back, possibly because some of his cancer cells had adapted to crizotinib. Dr. Ross Camidge at the University of Colorado Hospital gave him an experimental "second-generation" drug. As of 2013, Matt is cancer-free. He left medical school and is now a doctoral student in the molecular medicine program at Cleveland Clinic's Lerner Research Institute. He studies the genetic basis for disease, hoping to further the knowledge that saved his own life. "I am a walking testament to the power of personalized medicine," he says. "There was no need to put me through broad chemotherapy. The drugs I received targeted [my cancer] perfectly."

According to Dr. Bolwell, Matt's story illuminates the value that personalized healthcare can deliver. But it also reveals the challenge that we're going to have in documenting it. "Five years ago, we would have tried chemotherapy for this patient that very probably would have done little to help him. With a molecular intervention, not only do we have a better clinical outcome, but we also avoid the expense of conventional chemotherapy. However, demonstrating the efficacy of personalized healthcare in a clinical trial is going to be extraordinarily difficult. Traditional clinical trials require large numbers of patients who are treated in a uniform way.

The very nature of personalized healthcare is such that you don't have large numbers of people readily available to you who have the same genetic abnormality. So we're going to have to develop different ways to perform genomic research. The whole clinical trial infrastructure and the way we've thought about these trials needs to change—and fast."

Dr. Bolwell cautions that genomics may not immediately bring easy cures for most kinds of cancer. "The good news is that there are more and more drugs in development. The bad news is that cancer treatment is really complicated." Cleveland Clinic oncologist Dr. G. Thomas Budd agrees. "Cancers are plastic. They change over time. Within a given cancer, there may be some common genetic abnormalities, but there are also cells that may develop other genetic abnormalities. There's a continual mutation that occurs in cancer, and some of those mutations will create drug resistance over time. That's the challenge. Given that, what we hope to do is transform cancer into a chronic disease by what we call 'molecular monitoring.' We hope to look at markers of the tumor circulating in the bloodstream and make treatment changes before the tumors grow and spread."

Ultimately, Dr. Bolwell is optimistic about the genomics' potential for improving the treatment of cancer. "The fact is that the field has to advance. For a very long time, chemotherapy and radiation were the only tools we had. They're very effective in some cancers, but for many, they're not as effective as we need them to be. I do think that the field of cancer therapy is migrating toward the genomic platform. It's possible that in 15 years, we'll be talking not about the anatomic location of the origin of cancer—breast cancer, pancreatic cancer, and so on—but rather about the genomic abnormalities associated with cancer. We'll reclassify how we look at cancers. Treatment for many cancers may not change overnight, but every little win is another brick in the wall, and the more bricks you have, the stronger your foundation for treating people successfully."

We can use personalized healthcare not only to develop and administer new treatments such as the one that Matt received through the use of genetic testing but also to tailor the delivery of existing treatments. Let's consider a condition that, while not usually a death sentence, can prove extremely debilitating: inflammatory bowel disease. It's called colitis if it's in the large intestine and Crohn's disease if it's in the small intestine. Most people with these diseases have very troubling symptoms, such as frequent diarrhea, abdominal pain, bleeding from the rectum, nausea, and weight loss. They are chronic diseases that have no cure. Fortunately, there are a number of treatments that can ease the inflammation and help people live a more ordinary life.

The problem is that some of these treatments can be too toxic for some people. As Cleveland Clinic gastroenterologist Dr. Bret Lashner explains, "One class of drugs causes 10 percent of patients who take them to experience dangerous reductions in their white blood cell counts. This leaves them susceptible to severe infections, such as pneumonia or tuberculosis." Personalized healthcare offers a solution. Before prescribing medications, doctors can now check how much of a certain enzyme people have in their bodies. This enzyme helps people metabolize the drugs. By measuring the enzyme level, doctors can determine the toxicity risk of the drug for each patient. "If we find that patients are at high risk of developing toxicity," Dr. Lashner says, "we'll start them at a relatively low dose and see how they tolerate it before we increase the dose."

Dr. Lashner sees personalized healthcare as a way to avoid the considerable patient discomfort and medical expenses that arise as a result of drug complications. "Years ago, I had a patient whose white blood cell count dropped to zero because of the drugs we gave her. I had to admit her to the hospital, and we had to be very careful about her exposure to infectious agents. This whole scenario could have been avoided if I had been able to measure her enzyme activity prior to giving her the medication. Now, we have that capability."

So far, in Dr. Lashner's specialty, there are few options for personalizing treatment in this way, but he believes that this will change. "I think research will progress so that we will be better able to treat our patients. We'll develop more markers to show who will benefit from certain therapies and who will develop toxicities. And there's no question that genomics can have this impact in other medical specialties as well. This is the way of the future."

Prostate cancer offers another exciting early example. It's well known that not all prostate cancers are the same. Some are aggressive, spreading to other organs and causing death in a couple of years. Others remain in the body for many years without spreading or causing serious health problems. A number of treatments exist, ranging from the surgical removal of the prostate to simple watchful waiting. At present, when doctors find evidence of prostate cancer, they have no way of knowing how serious the cancer is. Therefore, it is difficult for them to know how aggressively they should treat it. Researchers such as Dr. Eric Klein, chairman of Cleveland Clinic's Glickman Urological & Kidney Institute, are now using genomics to change that. They're investigating a new genetic test that can give men with prostate cancer a much better sense of whether they are likely to have an aggressive form of the cancer. Combining this test with a traditional clinical assessment can help more men feel confident about choosing watchful waiting—and avoiding the potential side effects of other treatments.

Engaging and Activating Patients

A third way in which personalization can add value in healthcare has to do with getting patients more involved in and engaged with their own care. In many areas of medicine, how well a patient does in a course of treatment depends in part on how consistently she takes medications or complies with other instructions given by her doctors. As Dr. Teng observes, "Some very preliminary evidence suggests that with some personal genomics testing and care that takes patients' preferences into account, patients become more motivated and more likely to follow through on the doctor's recommendations. The research is scattered, but it is perhaps strongest with regard to chronic diseases such as diabetes."

Diabetes patients seem to follow recommendations better when doctors take the patients' specific goals into account. At age 20, a diabetic might want to stay off insulin, whereas at age 50, that same patient might want to avoid a severe complication of diabetes, such as kidney disease. At age 80, a diabetic who has multiple health problems might just want to get off diabetes drugs and enjoy the best short-term quality of life. It seems logical that doctors who take the time to talk to individual patients and determine exactly what is important to them about their care will find their patients to be more cooperative and engaged.

Information about the genome can help too. One Cleveland Clinic patient was a severely overweight woman in her late thirties who was making little effort to lose weight or to exercise. In advance of her annual wellness check, we asked her to complete her family history using an online tool we have developed. The patient at first declined, saying it would be too much work. Her doctor persisted, suggesting that it would help in her care. The woman filled out the history, and the doctor then was able to show her a compelling family tree diagram. Her mother, her sister, and her brother all had diabetes. The patient, represented in the center of the diagram, was the only one who was unaffected. The doctor said, "What do I need to do to get you to understand your risk of diabetes and to make better lifestyle choices?" The patient broke down in tears. She said that she had never understood her situation in this way, in terms of a graphical depiction of her family. She vowed to make changes to improve her health and reduce her diabetes risk.

Bringing Genomics into Cleveland Clinic

When I became CEO, Cleveland Clinic had not yet embraced the potential of personalized healthcare. Over the past several years, we've been moving quickly. In 2005, we recruited Dr. Eng to found and lead the Genomic Medicine Institute. The idea was to create a single platform in our organization that would link basic genomic medicine research, clinical practice, and education. The clinical arm of the institute, the Center for Personalized Genetic Healthcare (CPGH), has a staff of genetic counselors—one of the largest in the country—that offers innovative diagnostic risk assessments and clinical tools for doctors to use. Unlike genetics programs at many other leading medical centers, CPGH applies genetics to all medical specialties—Alzheimer's disease, cancer, and more. Because we're an integrated group practice, CPGH is able to interface throughout our system, bringing genomics seamlessly to many of our community hospitals, family health centers, and clinics.

In 2011, we launched another initiative, our Center for Personalized Healthcare (CPH), in hopes of doing better at introducing personalized healthcare developments and integrating them across our system. We wanted to go beyond genomics and consider other elements such as patient preferences, beliefs, goals, and environmental exposures. CPH operates as our hub for the identification, analysis, adoption, and integration of new services and technologies that allow for personalized preventive care. The center provides doctors and nurses with the tools and resources they need to create genetically informed personalized care plans for their patients. CPH also provides information and tools for patients that empower them to participate proactively in the management of their health.

Over the past few years, the Genomic Medicine Institute and CPH have come together with our other institutes to introduce important innovations. One of these, the Personalized Medication Program (PMP), is an alert-based system that notifies clinicians of the recommendation that they order genetic testing when they are prescribing medicine. PMP was rolled out enterprisewide in 2013 and helps doctors prescribe certain medications and adjust the doses to decrease the risk of side effects and drug interactions. The system is also designed to avoid duplication in genetic testing, which helps prevent unnecessary cost.

Another innovation that we've created, MyFamily, is the world's first clinical decision support application that is made available through the existing electronic medical record system. The tool is designed to systematize and automate the old-fashioned manual collection and use of family history. We've all had the experience of going to the doctor and sitting there with a clipboard trying to remember what illness our Aunt Edna or our Cousin Eddie had. Sometimes doctors use that information, and sometimes they don't. MyFamily is a custom-built software tool that identifies patients who have upcoming wellness check appointments and asks them to participate in a previsit information-gathering process. Patients are queried about the health history of their parents, their grandparents, and their own children. The easy-to-use online collection system makes it possible for patients to save their work so that they can return to it later if they need to find answers or gather additional family information. The ability for patients to input data on their terms—in their homes and at their own pace—supports our Patients First mission.

Once the patient tells the system that he has finished entering data, the data are sent to a pedigree-drawing tool that builds a concise pedigree image, which is then attached to the patient's electronic medical record for future reference. In addition, MyFamily uses a set of highly tuned proprietary algorithms to stratify the patient's risk for disease. At the time of the clinical encounter, the clinician is presented with these findings and may act on them in a number of ways, such as by undertaking recommended screening, behavior modification, or other preventive care. This tool allows our clinicians to bypass the collection of family history and spend their precious face-to-face time with patients actually counseling them, developing preventive care plans, and directing them to appropriate screening or consultations based on risk.

In practice, primary care doctors who suspect that a patient could have an inherited condition may not have the time to provide comprehensive genetic counseling and risk assessment. In these cases, the Center for Personalized Genetic Healthcare can step in to devote as much time to risk assessment and counseling as a patient needs. The center's physicians and genetic counselors offer the referring doctor a full report on their findings and help patients identify the most appropriate genetic test. "Because of the complexity of genetics and genomics," says Dr. Rocio Moran, a clinical geneticist at Cleveland Clinic, "we need to be available to explain a patient's test results. We will spend an hour or two with the patient and family members and discuss the full implications of what we've learned and what it could mean for them."

MyFamily currently provides risk assessment and clinical decision support for many diseases, including hereditary and familial cancers, and common conditions such as diabetes. As of 2013, the system performs more than 3,400 risk assessment calculations for each submitted health history. Still other algorithms are under development. During the pilot phase, only specific clinicians at Cleveland Clinic (and their patients) could use MyFamily. As of 2013, having successfully completed the pilot, we are working to make MyFamily available systemwide. We see it as an important step toward a healthcare system that personalizes the care it offers. Given the intense collaboration required to develop, test, and implement MyFamily, it's also an innovation that exemplifies the benefits of our large, physician-led group practice model.

The government does not yet reimburse us for a tool such as MyFamily, but we hope it will do so someday as MyFamily's clinical value becomes more widely accepted. We have already seen this value play out firsthand. In one case, a Cleveland Clinic physician had been seeing a man in his early fifties for more than 10 years. The physician had known that heart disease ran in this man's family and that the man's mother had died of ovarian cancer when she was in her forties. The patient was also of Ashkenazi Jewish ancestry, which greatly increases the risk for ovarian cancer due to the *BRCA* gene mutation. MyFamily flagged the patient for genetic testing—despite the fact that this patient was male. Why? Because in men, the *BRCA* gene mutation also increases the risk for prostate, breast, and skin cancer. "I knew this patient very well," the physician said. "I just never knew he needed to go and see a genetic counselor and have the testing done. I hadn't put all the pieces together." Since the patient had two adult daughters, genetic testing would probably yield information that would affect their health too.

So far, all indications are that doctors and patients love MyFamily and the personalization of care that it affords. Dr. Daniel Sullivan is a primary care physician in one of Cleveland Clinic's family health centers. He and his nurse-practitioner piloted MyFamily in 2012 and now use it regularly in his practice. "I expect the use of MyFamily to spread quickly. The program allows patients to take some ownership of their family history. They start calling family members to track down information, and this makes them feel like a partner in their own care. Not surprisingly, they seem more inclined to work with us on problems such as obesity, diabetes, and high blood pressure. It's a huge benefit. Meanwhile, I can make sure that they get the screenings and other preventive care that they need."

Dr. Sullivan describes one patient who came in with a family history of colon cancer. The common practice is to screen for the illness with colonoscopies starting at age 50. Dr. Sullivan advised his patient to get a colonoscopy at a younger age. The test was done, and the patient was found to have precancerous polyps. By having these removed, the patient was probably prevented from developing cancer. "Having rigorous family history information can dramatically improve the patient's quality of life, and also the cost of treatment," Dr. Sullivan concludes. "We can't afford any longer just to treat diseases as they arise. We need to get much better at preventing them. It's the only way to bring costs down."

Personalized Medicine and You

In just a few years, Cleveland Clinic and other institutions have made important strides in personalizing the care we offer patients.

But we hope that this will be just the beginning. Leading health centers all around the country are investing in genomics.[11] I can imagine a day in the not-too-distant future when we test children for their genetic profile at a very young age and this lets us understand everything they'll need to do throughout their lives to prevent disease and enjoy optimum health. Within the next 5 to 10 years, I think we'll see more electronic systems like MyFamily that will incorporate personalized information and bring it to the point of care in useful ways. We'll see more advances in the genomic treatment of specific illnesses. As others have argued, we might also see a wide array of genetic tests available over the counter in drugstores, as well as counseling centers where patients will be able to learn which drugs will work best given their personal genetic signature.[12]

There are many things that you as a patient can do right now to begin taking advantage of personalized healthcare. Work on becoming a true partner in your own individualized healthcare. Ask your healthcare provider questions about increased risk factors for certain conditions based on your family history, clarification of the diagnosis, and treatment options. Inform healthcare providers about your family health history, lifestyle, and environment. Family health history is among the most practical and effective tools that doctors can use to help them assess patients and identify those who are at risk for genetic and inheritable conditions. Act responsibly by following your provider's medication regimens, keeping scheduled appointments, and making healthy lifestyle decisions. These simple modifications enable doctors to practice proactive medicine (preventive care) rather than reactive medicine (acute care). Also, consider being tested to learn about your genetic makeup and receive an evaluation by a genetics professional.[13]

The medical advances we've seen over the past century are truly stunning, but we're only just beginning to unravel the molecular basis of life. A century of discovery awaits us, and, with it, higher-value healthcare for all.

Toward a Healthier Future

There are interconnected trends that are shaping twenty-first-century medicine: the movements toward large group practices, collaboration, use of big data, innovation, better patient experience, wellness and integrated care, and personalized medicine. Our healthcare system has the potential to be much better, more efficient, and more affordable than it is today. We have it in our power to make healthcare work, but for that to happen, we need to push these trends further—as professionals, as patients, and as Americans. We need to make healthcare bigger and more efficient, but simultaneously smaller, more intimate, more personal, and more suited to the individual patient, so that it serves us well and delivers *value*.

American medicine stands at a crossroads. Questions about finance, regulation, and the organization of medical services hover at the forefront of our national discussion. How we answer these questions will affect the lives and health of millions of people in the years to come. We face major challenges, yet I feel strongly optimistic about the future of healthcare in America.

Society faces a public health crisis of unimaginable proportions in the coming years. Breakthroughs in the treatment of infectious diseases, improvements in public health, and continuing innovation in cardiac surgery, orthopedics, stroke treatment, and emergency care have allowed Americans to live longer than ever. Fewer people are dying young of heart attacks, polio, measles, or pneumonia, but now our hospitals and medical centers are filling up with a whole set of different and, in many ways, more stubborn disease conditions. Three factors are driving this.

A Rapidly Aging Population

According to the Administration on Aging, more than 40 million Americans are currently aged 65 or older. By 2030, the number of Americans who are over 65 will have more than doubled from their number in 2000, to almost 20 percent of the population. Among today's older adults, most have at least one chronic disease, and at least one in four has two or more. The world financial crisis of 2008 and other factors make it likely that our older demographic will be an increasingly poorer demographic. Poverty will raise older people's already high risk for disease and disability and shift the cost of care almost entirely from the individual to society.

Preventable Diseases

Smoking, overuse of alcohol, poor diet, lack of physical activity, and chronic anxiety are promoting some of the most serious, destructive, and expensive diseases that we treat. Type 2 diabetes, hypertension, cardiovascular disease, and many types of cancer are not mysterious diseases that come out of nowhere. They are largely caused by our own lifestyle choices. Most people have at least a vague understanding of the cause-and-effect relationship between lifestyle and disease, but they lack the self-discipline or motivation to change their behavior.

Diseases of the Aging Brain

Advances in medicine are helping Americans live longer than ever. That's the good news. The bad news is that our bodies are outliving our brains, and we're increasingly suffering from Alzheimer's disease and other age-related neurodegenerative diseases. Alzheimer's currently affects an estimated 5.2 million people, costs the nation about $200 billion, and is the sixth leading cause of death. Doctors aren't really sure what causes the disease, but they do know that Alzheimer's shares major risk factors with cardiovascular disease, such as high cholesterol, obesity, smoking, and a sedentary lifestyle.

As America's healthcare providers struggle to cope with a pandemic of chronic disease, they will also need to manage change in response to government legislation. We have no way of knowing how the Affordable Care Act will play out in the coming years. But we do know that we are moving from a volume-based to a value-based system of payment. Government, insurance companies, and other providers are going to reward those providers who are able to achieve the right balance among quality, outcomes, and cost, and they will penalize those who are unable to align their costs better with the healthcare outcomes that they produce. Pressure is mounting on healthcare providers to reorganize the delivery of care so that they can do far more with less.

But I am optimistic about the future of healthcare. I am not only optimistic but *powerfully and enthusiastically* optimistic about the future of healthcare, for a number of reasons.

First, the national discussion on healthcare reform has focused new attention on wellness and prevention. More and more people are seeking to avoid lifestyle diseases through nutritional counseling, exercise, and stress management techniques. Medical studies have shown that people who participate in comprehensive lifestyle modification programs can and do experience rapid, significant, and clinically meaningful improvement in their disease risk, physical health, and mood. Scores of hospitals, schools, businesses, and other organizations have contacted Cleveland Clinic to learn how we use employee health insurance incentives and free wellness tools to improve caregivers' health and lower our healthcare costs.

Second, the digital revolution is having a clear and powerful impact. There was a time when medical decision making was cloaked in secrecy. Patients weren't able to look at their medical records, and data on hospital outcomes, volumes, and mortality rates were not available, if they were collected at all. Today, you have access to all this and more. The Internet, the electronic medical record, and advanced medical imaging are wiping the film of secrecy from healthcare and letting the light shine in. Digital technology is also making doctors' work better and easier. The electronic medical record allows them to see at a glance the patient's medical history and medications, along with notes from other caregivers. And in the clinical arena, ultra-crisp 3D digital imaging has transformed diagnosis and treatment in everything from ophthalmology to aortic arch repair.

Health information technology leads naturally to a third reason for hope: the rise of evidence-based medicine. What really works in healthcare? What treatments make patients better? These seem like obvious questions, but until recently, doctors and hospitals had little incentive to answer them systematically. Value-based healthcare is changing all that. Today's caregivers are engaged in an industrywide push to establish what works and what doesn't. The goal is to map out whole episodes of care, from admission to discharge and beyond, based on an agreed-upon set of best practices, with cost and patient experience factored in. If we can implement care paths across a broad spectrum of providers and get people to lose weight, exercise, and stop smoking, we have a good chance of lowering the cost of healthcare in our lifetimes.

Fourth, we are in the midst of a great consolidation of healthcare providers. Hospitals are merging their financial functions, information technology, and purchasing. There have been 170 hospital mergers over the past year. Today, 60 percent of the country's hospitals are part of a system. We're all getting more realistic about the costs of healthcare and who pays for it. The result will make medicine more efficient, effective, and accessible to all.

Our whole nation is about to wake up to a new world of healthcare. We are moving from the healthcare system of the 1950s to a system that is better suited to the twenty-first century. Yet in making this leap, we would be foolish not to build on the best of what has come before. Ninety years ago, four Cleveland physicians had a great idea for reducing healthcare costs. They established Cleveland Clinic as a not-for-profit group practice with a mission of patient care, research, and education. This model of medicine has made it possible for us to achieve cost savings on a vast scale. We know it is replicable. In fact, we have successfully transplanted our cultural DNA to Cleveland Clinic Florida, in Weston, and, very soon, to Cleveland Clinic Abu Dhabi. This is one more reason that I'm optimistic—because a powerful and proven model for surviving amid the new realities already exists. We don't have to reinvent the wheel but rather embrace and apply the wisdom of our forebears.

The founders of Cleveland Clinic were relentless in their drive to find a way to do things better. Now it's our turn. Healthcare professionals, policy makers, patients, and citizens together can lead the way to improved healthcare delivery in this country. I've written this book in the hope of creating a movement of individuals who realize what is at stake and what is possible and who are committed to leading the way. Count yourself as a member of this movement. Speak out about healthcare. Break new ground. Make new connections. Be a pioneer.

Join my colleagues and me in embracing the Cleveland Clinic Way. This approach to healthcare doesn't have to belong solely to us. It can belong to you, too. Our entire country will be healthier for it.

History of Cleveland Clinic: A Timeline

1891

Dr. George Crile, Sr., and Dr. Frank Bunts combine their resources to buy the surgical practice of the late Dr. Frank Weed.

1895

Dr. William Lower joins the growing practice.

1914–1918

Dr. Crile, Dr. Bunts, and Dr. Lower go overseas to serve in military hospitals during World War I. Inspired by military teamwork, they make plans to found a new kind of medical center in Cleveland when the war is over.

1921

Dr. Crile, Dr. Bunts, Dr. Lower, and a new partner (also a military veteran), Dr. John Phillips, open Cleveland Clinic as a not-for-profit multispecialty group care organization to provide patient care, research, and education. Dr. William Mayo delivers the keynote address at the dedication of the new offices on February 26, 1921.

1921–1928

Cleveland Clinic flourishes. A 140-bed hospital, laboratories, and a pioneering diabetes treatment unit are built. Patients and visitors include William Randolph Hearst, Charles Lindbergh, and government officials from the United States and abroad.

1929

Volatile nitrate films stored in the basement of the outpatient clinic ignite and release a cloud of poison gas into the building. Heroic and self-sacrificing actions by caregivers and first responders save lives, but 123 patients, visitors, and caregivers die from gas inhalation. Cleveland Clinic rises from the ashes as a leader in quality, safety, and preparedness.

1932

The *Cleveland Clinic Quarterly* (now the *Cleveland Clinic Journal of Medicine*) begins.

1941

During the Great Depression, Cleveland Clinic doubles in size to 740 caregivers, including doctors, nurses, and support personnel.

1942

Cleveland Clinic's Naval Reserve Unit establishes Mobile Hospital No. 4 in the South Pacific theater of war.

1948

Dr. Maurice M. Rapport, Dr. Arda Green, and Dr. Irvine Page isolate and name serotonin, now known to be an important neurotransmitter.

1950–1966

Dr. Willem Kolff, inventor of the kidney dialysis machine, refines and improves the device at Cleveland Clinic.

1954

Cleveland Clinic continues to grow. A new hospital building doubles the number of beds.

1955

The organization's first physician-led board of governors is chosen, ending a period of mixed physician and lay administration and beginning a new era of physician leadership.

1956

Cleveland Clinic surgeons perform one of the world's first stopped-heart surgeries, using a heart-lung machine developed in partnership with local industry.

1957

Dr. Kolff, head of artificial organs research, implants the first completely artificial heart in a lab animal.

1958

Dr. F. Mason Sones discovers selective coronary cineangiography at Cleveland Clinic, making possible the modern era of coronary intervention worldwide.

1963–1967

Cleveland Clinic surgeons led by Dr. Ralph Straffon report the success of cadaver kidney transplants, vastly increasing the potential donor pool.

1968

Dr. René Favaloro publishes the world's first reported coronary artery bypass surgery. Cleveland Clinic's pioneering cardiac surgery program gains new prominence.

1972–1984

Cleveland Clinic's growing reputation in all specialties brings an increasing number of patients. They come from surrounding communities, all 50 states, and around the world. Patients include world leaders, business leaders, sports figures, and celebrities.

1985

A major expansion is completed. It includes a new outpatient building designed by Cesar Pelli, new hospital facilities, and a two-block-long skyway linking the greatly enlarged campus.

1986

Leading Cleveland Clinic cardiac surgeons publish a key paper documenting the 10-year survival rates of patients having coronary artery bypass using an internal mammary artery graft. The report draws from information in the Cleveland Clinic's pioneering computerized cardiovascular patient registry.

1988

Cleveland Clinic Florida opens in Fort Lauderdale.

1989

Dr. Floyd D. Loop is appointed chairman of the board of governors.

1990

Cleveland Clinic is ranked number one in urology and digestive diseases in the first *U.S. News & World Report* hospital rankings.

1993

Cleveland Clinic opens the first of what by 2013 were a total of 16 full-service family health centers in surrounding communities. This is the beginning of the integrated regional healthcare delivery system.

1995

Cleveland Clinic is ranked number one in heart and heart surgery in *U.S. News & World Report* and continues to be number one every year through the present.

1996

Dr. C. Martin Harris is named Cleveland Clinic's first chief information officer and begins the transition from paper to electronic medical records.

1997

Cleveland Clinic begins merging with local hospitals, launching what will be by 2013 a system of eight Cleveland Clinic community hospitals.

1999–2004

Cleveland Clinic opens the Lerner Research Institute building, the Cole Eye Institute, the Taussig Cancer Center, and the Center for Genomics Research on its main campus.

2001

Cleveland Clinic Florida opens an integrated medical campus in Weston, Florida.

2002

Cleveland Clinic is ranked number three overall among the nation's best hospitals in *U.S. News & World Report.*

2002

Cleveland Clinic Lerner College of Medicine is established to train a new generation of clinician investigators.

2004

Dr. Toby Cosgrove is named president and CEO of Cleveland Clinic.

2005

Cleveland Clinic bans smoking on all its properties.

2007

The Office of Patient Experience is launched and the first chief experience officer is appointed.

2007

Only nonsmokers are hired.

2007

Cleveland Clinic reorganizes its medical and surgical departments and support services into 27 patient-centered institutes centered on specific diseases and body systems.

2008

Cleveland Clinic offers its caregivers free weight-loss programs and fitness center memberships on the employee health plan.

2008

The Miller Family Pavilion and Glickman Tower open on the main campus, adding 1 million square feet and 100 new beds for the Miller Family Heart & Vascular Institute and the Glickman Urological & Kidney Institute.

2008–2012

Cleveland Clinic caregivers working in doctor-led teams reduce operating expenses by $150 million while improving the quality and safety of patient care.

2009

President Barack Obama praises the Cleveland Clinic model of medicine in a national address and visits Cleveland Clinic to "show why their system works so well."

2010

The Cleveland Clinic Lou Ruvo Center for Brain Health opens in Las Vegas, Nevada.

2012

Cleveland Clinic enjoys one of its best years ever, with more than 5 million patient visits and 1 million same-day appointments. Total operating revenues increase, and community benefit exceeds the national average.

Notes

Preface

1   This story was taken from a Cleveland Clinic promotional patient video and follow-up interview with Terri McCort conducted January 15, 2013.

Chapter 1

1   Aaron Young, Humayun J. Chaudhry, Jon V. Thomas, and Michael Dugan, "A Census of Actively Licensed Physicians in the United States 2012," *Journal of Medical Regulation* 99, No. 2, p. 13.

2   Accenture, "Clinical Transformation: New Business Models for a New Era in Healthcare," September 27, 2012, http://www.accenture.com/us-en/Pages/insight-new-business-models-new-era-healthcare-summary.aspx.

3   Suzanne M. Kirchhoff, "Physician Practices: Background, Organization, and Market Consolidation," Congressional Research Service, January 2, 2013, http://www.fas.org/sgp/crs/misc/R42880.pdf.

4   Grace Crile, ed., *George Crile: An Autobiography*, Vols. 1 and 2 (Philadelphia and New York: J. B. Lippincott Co., 1947).

5   Portions of this section appeared initially in John D. Clough, ed., *To Act as a Unit: The Story of the Cleveland Clinic*, 5th ed. (Cleveland, Ohio: Cleveland Clinic Foundation, 2011).

6   Lawton R. Burns, Jeff C. Goldsmith, and Ralph W. Muller, "History of Physician-Hospital Collaboration: Obstacles and Opportunities," in Kaiser Permanente Institute for Health Policy, *Partners in Health: How Physicians and Hospitals Can Be Accountable Together*, ed. Francis J. Crosson and Laura A. Tollen (San Francisco: Jossey-Bass, 2010).

7   Clough, ed., *To Act as a Unit*.

8   Palo Alto Medical Foundation, "A Brief History of Group Practice," http://www.pamf.org/about/pamfhistory/grouppractice.html, accessed August 24, 2013.

9   Kaiser Permanente Institute for Health Policy, *Partners in Health: How*

Hospitals and Physicians Can Be Accountable Together, ed. Francis J. Crosson and Laura A. Tollen (San Francisco: Jossey-Bass, 2010).

10   Clough, ed., *To Act as a Unit.*

11   Quoted in Lawrence P. Casalino et al., "Benefits of and Barriers to Large Medical Group Practice in the United States," *Archives of Internal Medicine,* Vol. 163 (2003), pp. 1958–1964.

12   President Barack Obama, weekly radio address, June 6, 2009, http://www.whitehouse.gov/the-press-office/weekly-address-president-obama-outlines-goals-health-care-reform.

13   Palo Alto Medical Foundation, "Brief History of Group Practice."

14   W. B. Weeks, D. J. Gottlieb, D. E. Nyweide, et al., "Higher Healthcare Quality and Bigger Savings Found at Large Multispecialty Medical Groups," *Health Affairs (Millwood)* 29, no. 5 (2010): 991–997.

15   Laura Tollen, "Physician Organization in Relation to Quality and Efficiency of Care: A Synthesis of Recent Literature," Commonwealth Fund, April 17, 2008, http://www.commonwealthfund.org/Publications/Fund-Reports/2008/Apr/Physician-Organization-in-Relation-to-Quality-and-Efficiency-of-Care--A-Synthesis-of-Recent-Literatu.aspx.

16   Randall D. Cebul, James B. Rebitzer, Lowell J. Taylor, and Mark E. Votruba, "Organizational Fragmentation and Care Quality in the U.S. Health System," *Journal of Economic Perspectives,* Vol. 22, No. 4 (Fall 2008): 93-113.

17   E. D. Hixson, S. Davis, S. Morris, and A. M. Harrison, "Do Weekends or Evenings Matter in a Pediatric Intensive Care Unit?" *Pediatric Critical Care Medicine* 6, no. 5 (2005): 523–530.

18   "Central Line Associated Bloodstream Infections (CLABSI) Acquired While in Intensive Care Units," January 2013, http://my.clevelandclinic.org/about-cleveland-clinic/quality-patient-safety/performance-reports/cleveland-clinic-main-campus.

19   E-mail from Marie Budev, medical director, Lung Transplantation, Cleveland Clinic.

20   Geisinger Health System, "2011 System Report," http://www.geisinger.org/about/2011_AR_FINAL.pdf.

21   R. A. Miki, M. E. Oetgen, J. Kirk, et al., "Orthopaedic Management Improves the Rate of Early Osteoporosis Treatment After Hip Fracture: A Randomized Clinical Trial," *Journal of Joint and Bone Surgery* 90, no. 11 (2008): 2346–2353.

22   B. C. James and L. A. Javits, "How Intermountain Trimmed Health Care Costs Through Robust Quality Improvement Effort," *Health Affairs* 30, no. 6 (2011): 1185–1191.

23 Cebul et al., op. cit.

24 Diane Suchetka, "Cleveland Clinic Vascular Medicine Doctor Heather Gornik Puts Listening First," *Plain Dealer*, January 13, 2013. This account draws heavily from Ms. Suchetka's article.

25 2012 Physician Retention Survey from Cejka Search and the American Medical Group Association (AMGA), figure cited in online press release, "Physician Turnover Hits New High as Housing and Stock Markets Recover," www.prnewswire.com, accessed October 1, 2013.

26 Delos Cosgrove, Michael Fisher, Patricia Gabow, et al., "A CEO Checklist for High-Value Health Care," Institute of Medicine, June 5, 2012, http://www.iom.edu/Global/Perspectives/2012/CEOChecklist.aspx.

27 Geisinger Health System, "2011 System Report."

28 James and Javits, "How Intermountain Trimmed Health Care Costs."

29 Cosgrove et al., "A CEO Checklist for High-Value Health Care."

30 Mark Froimson, "In-Home Care Following Total Knee Replacement," *Cleveland Clinic Journal of Medicine* 80, e-Supplement no. 1 (2013): eS15–eS18.

31 Press release, "Walmart Expands Health Benefits to Cover Heart and Spine Surgeries at No Cost to Associates," October 11, 2012, http://news.walmart.com/news-archive/2012/10/11/walmart-expands-health-benefits-to-cover-heart-spine-surgeries-at-no-cost-to-associates.

32 Hospitals can be compared across numerous domains at this site: http://www.medicare.gov/hospitalcompare.

Chapter 2

1 Jay Crosson, "Patient Safety and the Group Practice Advantage," *The Permanente Journal* 5, no. 3 (2001): 3–4.

2 Thomas Bodenheimer, "Coordinating Care—A Perilous Journey Through the Health Care System," *New England Journal of Medicine*, vol. 358, no. 10 (2008): 1064–1071.

3 Ibid.

4 John Clough, ed., *To Act as a Unit: The Story of the Cleveland Clinic*, 4th ed. (Cleveland, Ohio: Cleveland Clinic Press, 2005), 27.

5 Ibid.

6 Ibid., 29.

7 A. A. Ghaferi, J. D. Birkmeyer, and J. B. Dimick, "Variation in Hospital Mortality Associated with Inpatient Surgery," *New England Journal of Medicine* 361, no. 14 (2009): 1368–1375.

8 D. M. Cosgrove 3d, J. H. Petre, J. L. Waller, J. V. Roth, C. Shepherd, and L. H. Cohn, "Automated Control of Postoperative Hypertension: A Prospective,

Randomized Multicenter Study," *Annals of Thoracic Surgery* 47, no. 5 (1989): 678–682.

9 Michael Porter, "A Strategy for Health Care Reform: Toward a Value-Based System," *New England Journal of Medicine* 361, no. 2 (2009): 109–112.

10 Michael Porter and Elizabeth Teisberg, *Redefining Health Care: Creating Value-Based Competition on Results* (Cambridge, Mass.: Harvard Business Review Press, 2006):105.

11 "America's Best Hospitals," *U.S. News & World Report*, 2012.

Chapter 3

1 Karin Connelly, "To Accommodate Rapidly Growing Staff, Explorys Moves into Former Museum Space," February 7, 2013, http://www.fresh watercleveland.com/features/explorysmove020713.aspx.

2 Explorys website, http://www.explorys.com, accessed August 27, 2013.

3 David Levin and Nicholas Molley, "Using and Managing Information Technologies," course offered at the Samson Global Leadership Academy for Healthcare Executives, Cleveland Clinic.

4 Robert E. Henkin and Jay A. Harolds, "Health Information Technology and the Electronic Medical Record," *Clinical Nuclear Medicine* 35, no. 10 (2010): 788–789.

5 Delos Cosgrove, Michael Fisher, Patricia Gabow, et al., "A CEO Checklist for High-Value Health Care," Institute of Medicine, June 5, 2012, http://www.iom.edu/Global/Perspectives/2012/CEOChecklist.aspx.

6 Devin Leonard and John Tozzi, "Why Don't More Hospitals Use Electronic Health Records?" http://www.businessweek.com, June 21, 2012.

7 Bruce Japsen, "Less than Two Percent of Hospitals Are Paperless as Medicare Penalties Loom," http://www.forbes.com, January 16, 2013.

8 Leonard and Tozzi, "Why Don't More Hospitals Use Electronic Health Records?"

9 "AMA Calls for Standardized Patient Records, Better Nutrition in Prisons," Reuters Health Medical News, June 22, 2011.

10 Henkin and Harolds, "Health Information Technology and the Electronic Medical Record."

11 Emily P. Walker, "EHR Adoption Way Up in Hospitals," medpagetoday.com, February 17, 2012.

12 Leonard and Tozzi, "Why Don't More Hospitals Use Electronic Health Records?"

13 Anne Scheck, "An Electronic Medical Record for a New Era," *Emergency Medicine News* 32, no. 5 (2010): 12–13.

14 Ibid.

15 F. D. Loop, B. W. Lytle, D. M. Cosgrove, et al., "Influence of the Internal-Mammary-Artery Graft on 10-Year Survival and Other Cardiac Events," *New England Journal of Medicine* 314, no. 1 (1986): 1–6.

16 Visit http://www.lerner.ccf.org/qhs/risk_calculator/.

17 Kevin B. O'Reilly, "ICU Central-Line Infections Drop Dramatically Nationwide," http://www.amednews.com, March 14, 2011.

Chapter 4

1 U.S. Department of Health and Human Services, Food and Drug Administration, "Innovation or Stagnation: Challenge and Opportunity on the Critical Path to New Medical Products," March 2004.

2 David Cassak, "Cleveland Clinic Innovations: Creating a Global Innovation Engine," *In Vivo* 30, no. 7 (2012): http://www.bioenterprise.com/resources/uploaded/InVivoArticle_1f2b.pdf.

3 "Innovation, the Challenge of Continual Newness", http://www.elearnspace.org/Articles/innovation.htm, accessed October 1, 2013.

4 MS statistics, National Multiple Sclerosis Society, www.nationalmssociety.org, accessed August 25, 2013.

5 Press release, "Renovo Neural Initiates First Dedicated Commercial 3D-Electron Microscopy Service; Collaborates with Customers to Co-develop New 3D Nanohistology Applications," April 17, 2012, http://www.businesswire.com/news/home/20120417005515/en/Renovo-Neural-Initiates-Dedicated-Commercial-3D-Electron-Microscopy.

6 Ibid.

7 "Cleveland Clinic Spinoff Renovo Neural Aims for Better Multiple Sclerosis Drug," May 17, 2011, medcitynews.com.

8 Quoted in Cassak, "Cleveland Clinic Innovations."

9 Andrew I. Schafer, ed., *The Vanishing Physician-Scientist?* (Ithaca, NY: ILR Press, 2009).

Chapter 5

1 Mohammadreza Hojat et al., "Empathy and Health Care Quality," *American Journal of Medical Quality* 28, no. 1 (2013): 6–7.

2 Quoted in Evelyn Theiss, "Patient Experience Summit Emphasizes Empathy and Engagement by Caregivers," May 22, 2012, http://www.cleveland.com/healthfit/index.ssf/2012/05/patient_experience_summit_emph.html.

3   Information drawn from Cleveland Clinic patient testimonials.

4   Mohammadreza Hojat et al., "The Devil Is in the Third Year: A Longitudinal Study of Erosion of Empathy in Medical School," *Academic Medicine* 84 no. 9 (2009): 1182–1191.

Chapter 6

1   Centers for Disease Control and Prevention, June 5, 2013, http://www.cdc.gov/tobacco/data_statistics/fact_sheets/fast_facts/.

2   Centers for Disease Control and Prevention, April 27, 2012, http://www.cdc.gov/obesity/adult/defining.html.

3   World Health Organization, http://www.who.int/countries/usa/en/.

4   Sarah Jane Tribble, "Initiatives Help Cleveland Clinic Employees Get Healthier, Lower Insurance Costs," *Cleveland Plain Dealer*, October 19, 2011.

Chapter 7

1   Peter Senge, *The Fifth Discipline: The Art and Practice of the Learning Organization*. New York, N.Y.: Currency Doubleday (1990), p. 7.

2   John F. Kennedy, "Address Before the Canadian Parliament in Ottawa," May 17, 1961, http://www.presidency.ucsb.edu/ws/?pid=8136.

Chapter 8

1   Angelina Jolie, "My Medical Choice," *New York Times*, May 14, 2013, http://www.nytimes.com/2013/05/14/opinion/my-medical-choice.html?_r=0.

2   "Getting Personal: The Promise of Cheap Genome Sequencing," *The Economist*, April 16, 2009. The cost of less than $10,000 in 2012 comes from the National Institutes of Health, National Genome Research Institute, http://www.genome.gov/sequencingcosts/.

3   In the interest of full disclosure, I must mention that my wife is director of strategic alliances at 23andMe Inc., a company that provides analyses of genetic material directly to consumers.

4   K. Teng, C. Eng, C. A. Hess, et al., "Building an Innovative Model for Personalized Healthcare," *Cleveland Clinic Journal of Medicine* 79, Suppl. 1, no. 4 (2012): S1–S9.

5   M. Doerr and C. Eng, "Personalised Care and the Genome," *BMJ* 344 (2012): e3174.

6   Taken from Charis Eng, "Harnessing the Human Genome Project for Value-Based Delivery of Healthcare," PowerPoint presentation, 2012, and

from Eric Klein, "PSA Screening for Prostate Cancer," PowerPoint presentation, Integrative Medicine and Wellness Summit, Chicago, 2010.

7   Charis Eng, "Molecular Genetics to Genomic Medicine Practice: At the Heart of Value-Based Delivery of Healthcare" (invited inaugural editorial commentary), *Molecular Genetics & Genomic Medicine* 1 (2013): 4–6.

8   B. Heald, T. Plesec, X. Liu, et al., "Implementation of Universal Microsatellite Instability and Immunohistochemistry Screening for Diagnosing Lynch Syndrome in a Large Academic Medical Center," *Journal of Clinical Oncology* 31, no. 10 (2013): 1336–1340.

9   "Asthma Genetic Risk Research Could Lead to Future Test," BBC, June 27, 2013, http://www.bbc.co.uk/news/health-23080636.

10   Matt Hiznay, "Matt Hiznay Is Changing the Face of Lung Cancer," http://www.teamdraft.org/survivorstories/matt-hiznay-is-changing-the-face-of-lung-cancer/, accessed September 4, 2013.

11   Anemona Hartocollis, "Cancer Centers Racing to Map Patients' Genes," *New York Times*, April 21, 2013.

12   "The Day of Precision Medicine Is Dawning, FDA Official Tells UMB," University of Maryland, March 10, 2009, http:/www.oea.umaryland.edu/communications/news/?ViewStatus=FullArticle&articleDetail=5835.

13   Jennifer Rainey Marquez, "Angelina Jolie's Decision: Should It Be Yours Too?" (interview with Dr. Charis Eng), *Parade*, May 14, 2013, http://www.parade.com/14174/jmarquez/angelina-jolies-decision-should-it-be-yours-too/.

Index

About the Author

Toby Cosgrove, MD, is president and chief executive officer of Cleveland Clinic. He presides over a $6 billion healthcare system that comprises Cleveland Clinic, 8 community hospitals, 16 family health centers, Cleveland Clinic Florida, the Lou Ruvo Center for Brain Health in Las Vegas, Nevada, Cleveland Clinic Toronto, and Cleveland Clinic Abu Dhabi. His leadership has emphasized patient care and patient experience, including the reorganization of clinical services into patient-centered, organ- and disease-based institutes. He has launched major wellness initiatives for patients, employees, and communities. Under his leadership, Cleveland Clinic has consistently been named among America's top four hospitals (*U.S. News & World Report*) and one of only two hospitals named among America's 99 Most Ethical Companies (Ethisphere Institute).

Dr. Cosgrove received his medical degree from the University of Virginia School of Medicine in Charlottesville and completed his clinical training at Massachusetts General Hospital, Boston Children's Hospital, and Brook General Hospital in London. His undergraduate work was at Williams College in Williamstown, Massachusetts.

He was a surgeon in the U.S. Air Force and served in Da Nang, Republic of Vietnam, as the chief of U.S. Air Force Casualty Staging Flight. He was awarded the Bronze Star and the Republic of Vietnam Commendation Medal.

Dr. Cosgrove joined Cleveland Clinic in 1975. He was named chairman of the Department of Thoracic and Cardiovascular Surgery in 1989. Under his leadership, Cleveland Clinic's heart program was ranked number one in America for 18 years in a row (*U.S. News & World Report*).

He has published nearly 450 journal articles and book chapters, 1 book, and 17 training and continuing medical education films. He performed more than 22,000 operations and earned an international reputation for expertise in all areas of cardiac surgery, especially valve repair. As an innovator, Dr. Cosgrove has 30 patents filed for developing medical and clinical products used in surgical environments.

Dr. Cosgrove has addressed the World Economic Forum annual meeting at Davos, Switzerland, and the Senate Health, Education, Labor, and Pensions Committee in Washington, DC. He is quoted and featured in national magazines and newspapers, including a cover story in *Time*, and major articles in *Newsweek*, the *New York Times*, and the *Washington Post*. He has appeared on CNN, Fox, MSNBC, NBC, CBS, *The Charlie Rose Show* on PBS, and other national media outlets.

The recipient of Cleveland Clinic's Master Clinician Award, Innovator of the Year Award, and Lerner Humanitarian Award, Dr. Cosgrove is also a member of the Cleveland Medical Hall of Fame and the Cleveland Business Hall of Fame. In 2007 he was named Cleveland Business Executive of the Year by the Sales and Marketing Executives of Cleveland, and Castle Connolly's National Physician of the Year. He also received the Woodrow Wilson Center Award for Public Service; Harvard Business School's Award from HBS Alumni, Cleveland; and the Humanitarian Award of the Diversity Center of Northeast Ohio. Dr. Cosgrove topped *Inside Business*'s "Power 100" listing for northeastern Ohio and is highly ranked among *Modern Healthcare*'s "100 Most Powerful People in Healthcare" and "Most Powerful Physician Executives."